SEX POSITIONS FOR MAGICAL MOMENTS

VICKY CROCKER

Contents

Chapter One

INTRODUCTION

Sex implies various things to various individuals. Most importantly, it is a sound and common movement. It is something a great many people appreciate and find meaningful regardless of whether they make meaning in various manners.

Whether you are straight, lesbian, gay, bisexual, eccentric, or questioning, you reserve the privilege to choose what sex intends to you.

If you are uncertain about your sexual interests? Is it true that you are interested in what you may appreciate? Is it true that you are wondering on the off chance that you are prepared for sex? These kinds of inquiries are consummately typical!

Sex isn't simply vaginal intercourse. Sex is basically anything that feels sexual. How YOU decide to define sex may be a moving objective during your high schooling years. Your sexual interests may change after some time, and that is alright too.

In the event that there's a tiny piece of you thinking "ouch" during sex, then it's an ideal opportunity to return to your bedroom technique. Sex ought to never be awkward, with the exception of perhaps in that entertainingly unbalanced manner. A few things in life are better on rehash: Friends, impeccably bright seashore days, your trusty white manicure. Your sexcapades, however? Definitely not one of them. Indeed, even the most sizzling sparkle in the bedroom needs new sex positions to stoke the blazes every now and then—Otherwise, things get boring, quick.

"Whenever you introduce something crisp and novel into the bedroom, you set yourself up for an all the more stimulating experience and greater finish.

Having sex just because with a new accomplice can be total firecrackers — or ungainly as hell-fire. However, having terrible sex, the first run through doesn't mean the sex will consistently be awful. You need to leave some room for individuals to become together. Once in a while, that just means working out their nerves; once in a while, it's getting to know one another, and once in a while, it's a straight-up discussion about the way that the sex isn't working.

In request to have a sound sex life, you have to have at times awkward discussions about what probably won't be working in the bedroom or what you need pretty much of."

On the off chance that it's not incredible in the beginning, there's actually no compelling reason to freeze. I've had some downright awful sex with individuals from the start that transformed into great sex later. I you are a very brave science, you can get the specialists directly with time. Ensure you're having an open discourse and stick to positions that aren't too muddled.

Tips to Improve Your Sex Life

How to Enjoy More Fulfilling Sex

Whether the issue is enormous or little, there are many things you can do to recover your sex life on track. Your sexual prosperity goes hand in hand with your general mental, physical, and enthusiastic wellbeing. Communicating with your accomplice, maintaining a solid way of life, availing yourself of a portion of the many fantastic self-improvement materials available, and simply having fun can assist you with weathering tough occasions.

Enjoying a satisfying sex life

Sex can bring out a kaleidoscope of feelings. From adoration, energy, and delicacy to longing, nervousness, and disappointment—the responses are as shifted as sexual encounters themselves. Also, many individuals will experience every one of these feelings and many others over the span of a sex life spanning quite a few years.

What is sex?

Sex is just one more hormone-driven considerable limit proposed to support the species. Clearly, that dainty view barely cares about the multifaceted idea of the human sexual response. Despite the biochemical forces at work, your experiences and wants assistance shape your sexuality. Your comprehension of yourself as a sexual being, your contemplations about what sets up a fantastic sexual affiliation, and your relationship with your accessory are key factors in your ability to make and keep up a satisfying sexual coexistence.

Talking to your accomplice

Many couples find it hard to discuss sex significantly under the best of conditions. At the point when sexual issues happen, feelings of hurt, disgrace, blame, and hatred can stop discussion altogether. Since great correspondence is a cornerstone of a solid relationship, establishing a discourse is the initial step not exclusively to superior sex life yet in addition to a closer, passionate bond. Listed are a few tips for tackling this delicate subject.

Locate the perfect time to talk. There are two sorts of sexual discourses: the ones you have in the room and the ones you have elsewhere. It's sublimely legitimate to specify to your assistant what feels extraordinary profoundly associated with lovemaking. Nonetheless, it's optimal for holding up until you're in a logically unprejudiced setting to discuss greater issues, for instance, mismatched sexual need or climax burdens.

Keep away from reprimanding. Couch recommendations in positive terms, for instance, "I really love it when you contact my hair gently that way," as opposed to concentrating on the negatives. Approach a sexual issue as an issue to be understood together instead of a movement in allocating shortcoming.

Trust in your associate about changes in your body. If sweltering flashes are keeping you up around night time or menopause has made your vagina dry, talk with your associate about these things. It's unfathomably improved that he understands what's really going on as opposed to decipher these physical changes as the nonattendance of intrigue. So also, in the event that you're a man and you never again get an erection just from sex, tell your associate the best way to enliven you as opposed to let her acknowledge she isn't adequately charming to animate you anymore.

Be clear. You may believe you're ensuring your accessory's sentiments by faking a climax, yet in fact, you're gazing intently at a slippery inclination. As trying for what it's worth to examine any sexual issue, the difficulty level skyrockets once the issue is secured under significant lots of deceptions, hurt, and scorn.

Make an effort not to compare love with sexual execution.

Make a quality of minding and delicacy; contact and kiss habitually. Make an effort not to blame yourself or your accessory for your sexual difficulties. Focus rather on keeping up eager and physical closeness in your relationship. For increasingly prepared couples, another possibly unstable subject that justifies talking about is what will happen after one assistant passes on. In couples who welcome a strong sexual coexistence, the enduring associate will most likely need to look out another assistant. Communicating your responsiveness to that believability while you are both still alive will presumably alleviate fault and make the method less hard for the enduring accessory later.

Utilizing personal growth approachs

Treating sexual issues is more straightforward now than whenever in ongoing memory. Dynamic medications and master sex advisors are there in case you need them. Nevertheless, you may have the choice to decide minor sexual issues by making a few changes in your lovemaking style. Listed are a few things you can try at home.

Educate yourself. A great deal of good personal development materials are available for every sort of sexual issue. Examine the Internet or your local book shop, select two or three resources that worry you, and use this tips to help you and your accessory become better educated about the issue. In the occasion that talking truly is excessively problematic, you and your associate can underline segments that you particularly like and demonstrate them to each other.

Security concerns and Internet use

The Internet is a significant wellspring of a wide scope of data, including books and different things (for instance, sex toys) that can improve your sexual coexistence. Regardless of the way that it may act naturally clear, never use your workplace PC to do such searches, to sidestep potential embarrassment with your director, who is likely prepared to pursue your request history. People who feel uneasy even about utilizing their home PCs and charge cards to orchestrate sex-related data or things online may have the choice to locate a near to store (especially in noteworthy urban networks) and pay with cash.

Give yourself time. As you age, your sexual responses deferred down. You and your associate can improve your chances of progress by finding a quiet, pleasing, without interference setting for sex. Furthermore, comprehend that the physical changes in your body infer that you'll require greater chance to get invigorated and land at climax. Exactly when you consider it, investing extra energy engaging in sexual relations is unquestionably not a terrible thing; working these physical exercises into your lovemaking routine can open up approaches to another sort of sexual experience.

Use oil. Consistently, the vaginal dryness that starts in perimenopause can be successfully reconsidered with greasing up liquids and gels. Use these energetically to avoid excruciating sex—an issue that can snowball into hailing drive and developing relationship pressures. Right when treatments never again work, analyze different choices with your primary care physician.

Keep up physical warmth. Notwithstanding whether you're depleted, tense, or upset about the issue, participating in kissing and nestling is essential for keeping up an energetic and physical bond.

Work on contacting. The sensate focus systems that sex advisors use can assist you with reestablishing physical closeness without feeling obliged. Numerous personal growth guides and informational chronicles offer a minor takeoff from these activities. You may in like manner need to demand that your accessory touch you in a way that the person being referred to should be contacted. This will give you an unrivaled sentiment of how a ton of weight, from fragile to firm, you ought to use.

Endeavor different positions. Building up a collection of different sexual positions adds enthusiasm to lovemaking, yet it can in like manner help overcome issues. For example, the expanded instigation to the G-perceive that happens when a man enters his associate from behind can empower the lady to land at climax.

The G-spot

The G-spot, otherwise known as Grafenberg spot, was named after the gynecologist who initially recognized it, is a slope of super-fragile spongelike tissue arranged inside the highest point of the vagina, essentially inside the path. Fitting actuation of the G-spot can convey extreme climaxes. In perspective on its difficult to-land at the region and how it is most successfully fortified physically, the G-spot isn't routinely activated for most women during vaginal intercourse. While this has driven a couple of critics to scrutinize its world, investigate has shown that a substitute sort of tissue exists around there.

You ought to be explicitly mixed to have the choice to discover your G-spot. To discover it, try focusing on your finger an enticing development along the highest point of your vagina while you're in a hunching down or sitting position, or have your accessory back rub the upper surface of your vagina until you notice a particularly fragile locale. A couple of women will, when all is said in done, be progressively fragile and can discover the spot adequately, yet for other people, it's irksome.

On the off chance that you can only with significant effort, find it, you shouldn't stress. During intercourse, many ladies feel that the G-spot can be most effectively invigorated when the man enters from behind. For couples dealing with erection issues, play involving the G-spot can be a positive expansion to lovemaking.

Oral incitement of the clitoris combined with manual incitement of the G-spot can give a woman a profoundly intense orgasm.

Record your dreams. This activity can assist you in exploring potential exercises you think maybe a turn-on for you or your accomplice. Take a stab at thinking of an encounter or a film that stirred you and then offer your memory with your accomplice.

Do Kegel exercises. The two people can improve their sexual wellness by exercising their pelvic floor muscles. To do these exercises, fix the muscle you would utilize on the off chance that you were trying to stop urine in midstream. Hold the withdrawal for a few seconds, then discharge. Rehash multiple times. Attempt to complete five sets per day. These exercises should be possible anyplace—while driving, sitting at your work area, or standing in a checkout line. At home, ladies may utilize vaginal loads to include muscle opposition. Converse with your doctor or a sex therapist about where to get these and how to utilize them.

Attempt to unwind. Accomplish something soothing together before having sex, for example, playing a game or going out for a decent dinner. Or then again attempt unwinding methods, for example, profound breathing exercises or yoga.

Utilize a vibrator. This gadget can enable a woman to find out about her own sexual reaction and enable her to show her accomplice what she loves.

Try not to surrender. On the off chance that none of your endeavors appear to work, don't surrender trust. Your doctor can frequently determine the reason for your sexual issue and might have the option to distinguish compelling medicines. The person in question can likewise place you in touch with a sex therapist who can assist you with exploring issues that might be standing in the method for fulfilling sex life.

Maintaining great wellbeing

Your sexual prosperity goes hand in hand with your general mental, physical, and passionate wellbeing. Therefore, the equivalent sound propensities you depend on to keep your body in shape can likewise get down to business your sex life.

Exercise, work out, and work out.

Physical movement is a matter of first importance among the solid practices that can improve your sexual functioning. Since physical excitement depends extraordinarily on great bloodstream, high-impact work out (which strengthens your heart and veins) is significant. And practice offers an abundance of other medical advantages, from staving off coronary illness, osteoporosis, and a few types of malignancy to improving your state of mind and helping you show signs of improvement night's rest. Additionally, remember to include quality training.

Make an effort not to smoke. Smoking adds to periphery vascular affliction, which impacts circulatory system to the penis, clitoris, and vaginal tissues. Moreover, women who smoke will, all in all, experience menopause two years sooner than their nonsmoking accomplices. If you need help stopping, endeavor nicotine gum or fixes or get some data about the drugs bupropion (Zyban) or varenicline (Chantix).

Exercise alcohol with some self-control. A couple of men with erectile brokenness find that having one beverage can empower them to loosen up, yet overpowering use of alcohol can intensify the circumstance. Alcohol can hinder sexual reflexes by dulling the central tangible framework. Drinking gigantic entireties over a broad stretch can hurt the liver, prompting an expansion in estrogen creation in most men. Alcohol can trigger hot flashes and upset rest in women, exacerbating issues successfully present in menopause.

Eat right. Overindulgence in oily sustenance prompts high blood cholesterol and weight—both critical peril factors for the cardiovascular disease. In addition, being overweight can propel slowness and poor self-recognition. Expanded moxie is regularly an extra bit of leeway of losing those extra pounds.

Use it or lose it. Exactly when estrogen drops at menopause, the vaginal dividers lose a segment of their versatility. You can slow this technique or even switch it through sexual development. If intercourse is certainly not a decision, masturbation is likewise as convincing, despite the way that for women, this is best if you use a vibrator or dildo (a thing looking like a penis) to help stretch the vagina. For men, broad stretches without an erection can preclude the penis from claiming a piece of the oxygen-rich blood that it is needed to keep up incredible sexual working. In this manner, something much the same as scar tissue makes in muscle cells, which meddles with the limit of the penis to grow when the circulatory system is expanded.

Putting the happiness again into sex

In reality, even in the best relationship, sex can become ho-mumble following different years. With a smidgen of creative mind, you can revive the radiance.

Be brave. Maybe you've never engaged in sexual relations on the family room floor or in a bound spot in the forested regions; directly might be a perfect chance to endeavor it. Or, then again, try investigating intriguing books and films. In reality, even just the sentiment of shrewdness you get from leasing a X-evaluated film may make you feel energetic.

Be arousing. Make a circumstance for lovemaking that interests to all of the five of your resources. Concentrate on the vibe of silk against your skin, the beat of a jazz tune, the perfumed scent of blossoms around the room, the sensitive point of convergence of candlelight, and the kind of prepared, scrumptious natural item. Use this expanded arousing care when making veneration to your accessory.

Be vigorous. Leave love notes in your accessory's pocket for the individual being referred to discover later. Wash up together—the warm, happy with feeling you have when you get away from the tub can be an unprecedented lead-in to sex. Tickle. Laugh.

Be innovative. Expand your sexual repertoire and shift your content. For instance, in case you're accustomed to making love on Saturday night, pick Sunday morning instead. Test with new positions and exercises. Attempt sex toys and sexy lingerie on the off chance that you never have.

Chapter Two

INTIMACY

Intimate connections exist between two individuals with physical or passionate closeness. While the term intimate relationship, for the most part, suggests the inclusion of sexual movement, the term is additionally used to indicate any association with something beyond sexual activity. Intimate connections maintain a key job in the general human experience since they involve passionate associations with others. This might be romance, physical or sexual fascination, sexual action, or passionate help, while additionally helping individuals create solid interpersonal associations.

All in all, the inquiry exists, "Are sex and intimacy various things?" We may likewise ask, "Would you be able to have one without the other? Or, on the other hand, does one lead to another?" There are many conflicting opinions on the jobs of sex and intimacy inside and outside of connections. Since no two individuals have similar thoughts on sex, there is no finite response to any of these issues. In a customary structure, sex includes long haul responsibility or marriage, trailed by passionate intimacy and reproduction. However, in an increasingly indiscriminate society, the association between sex and intimacy can be a questionable one.

Physical intimacy is portrayed by kinship, platonic love, romantic love, or sexual action. While there are distinct type of intimacy, physical inti-macy is just one of those. It is frequently about sex, however significantly more. Association and correspondence with others around us assemble physical intimacy, and regularly, fascination in somebody of the contrary sex is a key factor of physical intimacy.

The inclusion of physical intimacy in human sex-uality is another factor that requires thought. It is accounted for that a great many people want physical intimacy or the like in any event once in a while, being that it is a characteristic piece of human sexuality. Since this is frequently sensual touching of any kind, it requires a passage into an-other's close to home space, while it might be an enthusiastic or sexual act anyplace from an em-brace to a kiss or sexual intercourse. Enthusiastic or sensual touching of this sort helps in the arrival of oxytocin, dopamine, and serotonin, which diminishes pressure. Likewise, without physical intimacy, there are increased feelings of loneliness or trouble.

There are essential definitions accommodated the definition of physical intimacy, particularly including the definitions of other words that are a piece of the physical demonstrations of intimacy. While many of the ones that are essential definitions are not real sex, they are as yet touching and physical interaction.

It could be a few things or action words, most normally stroke or caress. There are additionally the equivalent words that depict these words, including stroke, snuggle, pet, grasp, embrace, nestle, pet, or pat. It appears to shift to and fro, particularly since there can be the inclusion of physical and passionate intimacy as a piece of an intimate relationship, making it not really a feeling or activity of its own.

While the different definitions of physical intimacy appear to reference sexual activities or passionate interaction or the like, that has all the earmarks of being progressively explicit of "physical." This is substantially more about touching, whether it be enthusiastic or sensual, implying that "physical intimacy," all in all, centers significantly more on the first of these two words.

Definition of Sexual Passion

Presently, this might be as straightforward as solace with individual warmth or with open presentations of friendship in view of the degree of intimacy that has created between two individuals. There is likewise the topic of whether there is sex or sexual passion without feeling or love, and whether it very well may be maintained.

If you are looking for the definition of sexual passion, many of indistinguishable references from physical intimacy showed up in various word reference areas. One extra notice is that of "friendship," something that is of expansion to the physical touching and intimacy that accompanies the feelings being communicated. While "love" and "love" are not totally the equivalent, this indicates there might be something more enthusiastic about the passionate side of this word combination.

Individuals who are close and natural are increasingly happy with entering each other's close to home space and taking on physical contact. Depending on the relationship, open presentations of warmth may differ dependent on the social standard in which they find themselves. These presentations can go from basic signals like a kiss or embrace to a grasp or holding hands. While this might be a basic greeting, there might be long haul contact or warm grasp maintained in the general population space when these two individuals are very alright with one another.

Then, there are strategies for contact that are maintained in private in a progressively intimate relationship. As two individuals become more like each other, they are calm and can show types of expressions of love when together, including:

These occasions don't require sexual movement to have passion or intimacy. However, this would probably indicate that it's anything but a sexually passionate relationship. In the event that two individuals are looking to maintain fellowship, it is more probable they will adhere to an embrace or kiss on the cheek to show care or fondness that isn't sexually passionate.

Therefore, physical, sexual intimacy can fluctuate in the definition. A few people are more sexually passionate than others and can bring that degree of intimacy into a romantic relationship considerably more effectively. There is additionally the way that every individual sees sex, in any event, a marginally unique manner, and usually, people address sexual intimacy and passion in an unexpected way.

Difference between Sex and Intimacy

Sex without affection or intimacy is an inquiry that exists at the center of any solid relationship. Since there is the estimation of sex between two individuals who have an intimate or loving relationship, there is likewise the significance of defining every single, distinctive bit of the relationship. General intimacy involves knowing somebody profoundly and the capacity to feel totally open, free, and fair with them. This is something that is ordinarily just felt or experienced with one individual, as this nearby intimacy is too hard to have with multiple individuals.

Along these lines, sex in a loving or intimate relationship will, in general, be the physical epitome of those feelings. The perfect theory is that this physical intimacy is to be a loving association between the two individuals in a relationship. Both of them within a relationship are in this way interconnected: physical intimacy manufactures sexual passion, and sexual passion constructs sexual intimacy.

There is the capacity to isolate sexual passion from physical intimacy too. This is if sex is only a physical demonstration, particularly when it happens outside of a relationship. Sex is the most intimate act. However, there are various events when this demonstration can happen. It tends to be a physical demonstration that happens without assent (assault), a demonstration that is paid for (prostitution), or a straightforward physical trade (one-night stand).

State that we consider the one-night stands that anybody takes on following a night of drinking or partying with companions. Any man or woman can appreciate a night of sex without affection or intimacy, for the most part, when there is physical fascination or the fundamental want for satisfaction in sexual intercourse. It is frequently a mental inquiry of the contrast between these two, and the general intimate and defenseless demonstration of offering yourself to another in sex, which would interface both sex and intimacy again.

When the determination of sexual passion or physical intimacy is made, there then comes the topic of sex or making love. With this having been a solid discussion for extensive stretches of time, there is the possibility to understand this is an independent choice to be made. Or, if nothing else, this would be the chosen term between the two accomplices who have set up their intimate, sexual relationship.

Since regardless of the term utilized, sex is constantly a physical demonstration and should be possible without intimacy. There is the potential for the love or intimacy involved in this demonstration to be a degree or level of association-related between the two accomplices involved, making it something that turns out to be progressively intimate or increasingly a type of lovemaking as their relationship develops after some time.

It is additionally critical to recall that loving and intimate couples now and again can't engage in sexual relations or decide not to do as such. There can be ailments that forestall sexual intercourse, making the physical intimacy in their relationship something of a milder level. This doesn't eliminate the passion or fascination they feel for each other. It likewise doesn't expel other types of physical intimacy and touching, or quality time spent together to express their affection and feelings for each other.

Intimacy is significant on the grounds that humans are social animals who flourish with close to home associations with others. While intimacy indicates pictures of romantic connections, it can likewise happen in dear kinships, parent-kid connections, and siblinghood. There are four sorts of intimacy:

- **Experiential Intimacy:** When individuals bond during relaxation exercises. Individuals may "synchronize" their activities in cooperation or find themselves acting like one.

Example: A father and child cooperate in manufacturing a model train, developing a cadence to their collaboration.

- **Emotional Intimacy:** When individuals have a sense of security, sharing their feelings with one another, even awkward ones.

Example: A woman trusts in her sister about her self-perception issues. She confides in her sibling to offer solace rather than using her insecurities against her.

- **Intellectual Intimacy:** When individuals feel great sharing thoughts and opinions, in any event, when they oppose this idea.

Example: Two companions banter the meaning of life. They appreciate hearing each other's opinions and don't want to "win" the contention.

- **Sexual Intimacy:** When individuals take part in sensual or sexual exercises. At the point when individuals utilize "intimacy," they are frequently referring to this sort.

Example: Two sweethearts take part in foreplay, knowing how each other likes to be touched.

Intimacy in a romantic relationship is normally something that is worked after some time. New connections may have snapshots of intimacy; however, building long haul intimacy is a steady procedure that requires persistence and correspondence. Many individuals judge the nature of their connections, dependent on the profundity of intimacy and how much they feel near their accomplices.

Approaches to Pursue Sexual Intimacy, Not Just Sexual Activity

As far as I can tell, as a clinical therapist, the couples who have the best sex are the individuals who really seek after blah. They understand that sexual intimacy is in excess of a sensual encounter. It is a voyage of development, articulation, and passion that can fashion their hearts in a manner that nothing else can.

Here are four things that can support you and your companion seek after sexual intimacy, not simply sexual movement.

Recollect intimacy is a long-distance race, not a sprint.

Our way of life has trained us to think about "extraordinary sex" as a flashing experience. It's about similarity and the passion existing apart from everything else. However evident sexual fulfillment isn't what occurs during a couple of sexual experiences, yet through the building and sustaining a long haul sexual relationship.

I regularly advise newlyweds to move toward sex as though they are opening up a case of Legos. In the event that they hope to find an amassed item, they will most likely be disappointed. The enjoy-ment of Legos is learning to turn into a specialist manufacturer. The enchantment is in the making. The equivalent is valid for sex. Intimacy results as a team figure out how to make extraordinary love with one another after some time. Indeed, even the impediments you face with your accomplice can be an invitation to learn and become togeth-er. Couples that have been hitched for a long time regularly state their sex life just continues getting better with time. Why? Since they have become specialists at communicating, resolving strife and learning each other's bodies. They have stored up recollections of chuckling and passion that make their intimate association meaningful.

Focus on growing and learning together.

Sexual intimacy doesn't simply occur; however, it results from investment. The huge thing you can do to construct sexual intimacy isn't done between the sheets. It is the promise to learn and speak with your accomplice.

Intimate couples are the individuals who have been in the channels together. They have tended to issues head-on instead of avoiding them. They talk about sexual enticements, wants, troubles, and wounds. They have constructed trust to share their most defenseless considerations and battles.

Guarantee never to utilize sex as a weapon.

In many connections, one individual has a more grounded sex drive than the other. After some time, couples create examples of interest and dismissal, evasion, and hatred. What was intended to fabricate intimacy turns into a ground-breaking weapon to partition.

One example is that one individual begins to demand sex from the other. Some may even cite the Bible, coercing through the message that "this is your obligation." In I Corinthians 7, the witness Paul expounds on the significance of sexual intimacy within marriage. However, we should recall that marriage was made to be a declaration of God's pledge love. As Paul composes later in that equivalent letter, "Love shows restraint, kind, doesn't look for its own specific manner." Married couples should make sexual intimacy a need, not simply having sex.

Intimacy requires trust and affectability to one another's necessities. When one individual uses sex to manipulate or rebuff the other individual, sex is never again about intimacy or love.

Make sexual intimacy a need.

Following an entire day of work, parenting, and everyday life, you're depleted. You fall into bed, eager to rest just to find that your accomplice is amped up for something else. Inwardly you moan, "Truly? Sex is on my mind." While this kind of sexual experience will undoubtedly be a piece of sex in marriage, it shouldn't be too visit. Having sex doesn't take a ton of vitality, yet sexual intimacy necessitates that you be completely present. This is one of the negatives of the individuals who urge individuals to say yes when a mate requests sex consistently. You begin to set up a propensity for sex around a sexual discharge rather than a sexual relationship. Actually, building sexual intimacy may mean saying "no" to sexual experiences that undermine relationship and trust.

Building sexual intimacy implies you make time to envision, to appreciate one another, to convey, and to go into the passion. It additionally necessitates that you work to address unsafe examples and triggers that prevent you from feeling sheltered and esteemed. This won't occur except if you proactively put aside time to manufacture intimacy.

The Peril of "No surprises Sex."

It is tragically amusing that our way of life speaks unendingly about sex, yet a great many people have never encountered the totality of what it was intended to be. Close to an incredible finish, he mirrored, "It's the way into my life, the need to feel adored... I think I've been searching to fill that gap that was left there in early adolescence. I think that what I'm likely doing is avoiding being harmed again. Security in larger groups."

The best hazard within a culture of "no hidden obligations sex" is that we become splintered individuals, believing that a physical demonstration can supplant the social and profound intimacy we long for... even within marriage.

Genuine Intimacy is More Than Sex

Possibly you are wondering about sex. Without a doubt, sex is a piece of intimate articulation. However, it isn't intimacy.

Sex can be the most intimate and excellent articulation of adoration; however we are possibly lying to ourselves when we go about as though sex is the verification of affection. Too many men demand sex as confirmation of adoration; too many ladies have given sex with expectations of affection. We live in a universe of clients where we misuse each other to dull the pain of aloneness. We as a whole long for intimacy and physical contact can show up as intimacy, in any event for a minute."

Genuine intimacy isn't discovered just by merging bodies in sex. At the point when Jesus stated, "And the two will get one. . . "I can't resist the urge to think that He implied something beyond the physical. All things considered, how many couples hit the hay around evening time, share their bodies, however not their hearts? Without a doubt, many of these individuals would state they are desolate. Why? Since similarly as a garden hose isn't the wellspring of water, however, just an articulation, or vehicle for it, so sex isn't the wellspring of intimacy, yet an outlet (or articulation of) it. Regardless of how hard you attempt, if genuine, enthusiastic, and otherworldly intimacy doesn't exist before sex, it assuredly won't after.

Genuine Intimacy Makes Us Feel Known

Genuine intimacy makes us feel alive like we've been found, as though somebody finally took an opportunity to look into the profundities of our spirit and truly observe us there. Up to that point, until we experience genuine intimacy, we will feel disregarded and overlooked, similar to somebody is looking directly through us.

Unfortunately, we can pass up an intimacy that can make us, and another individual feel is known when we predetermine what we think we should see when we examine their life, heart, character, and soul. At the point when this occurs, we will attempt to shape and cause them into who we to accept they ought to be. Therefore, we are blinded to their great characteristics, and love and intimacy are demolished.

Genuine Intimacy Begins With You

Maybe you are wondering how you can construct an intimate relationship. Notwithstanding accepting another individual exactly how they are, (Note: This doesn't mean accepting any type of misuse), genuine intimacy can just begin once you know yourself. Since intimacy signifies "in-to-me-see," how can anybody "see into" you and what your identity is, your feelings of dread, dreams, expectations, and wants except if you know what your identity is and are eager to permit somebody in? Experiencing genuine intimacy begins with being associated with your own heart.

Without a doubt, sharing who we are with others is regularly difficult. All adoration is a hazard. I concede, it very well may be awkward, exposing the deepest pieces of ourselves. Fortunately, you don't need to do it at the same time since developing intimacy resembles peeling an onion—it can happen only a little at once while trust is created.

Intimacy with God is real and rewarding

Since God made us, He intimately realizes us superior to anything anybody can. Therefore, He can make us feel known in a manner that nobody on earth is capable, and in this, we can encounter intimacy in an indescribable manner. Intimacy with God through His Son Jesus has been the most rewarding and groundbreaking thing I have ever experienced.

Sexual passion and relationship intimacy may debilitate after some time. For a few, it might have never been solid in any case. Some lose want towards sexual intimacy because of awful or negative encounters, relationship issues, aging, the irrelevance of relationship intimacy, or demeanors squeezed by others that make disgrace, blame, or aversion towards sexual intimacy. Now and then, the desires for one are strong to such an extent that their accomplices cannot meet them, leading to disappointment in one of the two accomplices and a lessening in sexual passion. It has been stated that the best wellspring of sensuality is at the command of the brain, so for the individuals who experience issues desiring relationship intimacy, here are some brain exercises that may increase want and sensuality.

Tune into your Senses

Become increasingly mindful of the vibes of your surroundings and encounters as an approach to increase want and sexuality. This strategy is something you can work on during consistently encounters. Slow down and appreciate shapes, hues, and lights; notice how they make you feel. Focus on the manner in which an article feels against the skin. Notice how sounds make a certain state of mind in you. Appreciate the kinds of your nourishment and the scents noticeable all around. Being in line with these sensations encourages you to be increasingly associated in the minute and to acknowledge what is pleasurable for you to encounter. Experiencing this kind of sensuality can serve to increase want towards relationship intimacy with your accomplice as you become on top of vibes that are aesthetical.

Indulge in Intimate Daydreams

To increase want, take some time every day to enable yourself to think about intimate interactions in a positive manner through daydreaming or fantasizing about intimate exercises that are appealing to you. Dreams are among you and yourself and ought not to be thought of as a genuine demonstration that you are performing around then. Fantasizing that you and your accomplice are in some spot quiet, excellent or intriguing to you, or that you two are portraying diverse character types (for instance, seeing the both of you in renaissance times, and so on), or to be touched/interacted with contrastingly or fantasizing of progressively unsafe or romantic circumstances might be sufficient to increase your sensuality in request to improve or expand your intimate associations and sensuality with your accomplice.

Investigate Sensations with your Partner

To increase want for relationship intimacy, set up a time where you and your accomplice experience sensuality together without sexual desires. For instance, for one night, invest energy touching one another, yet don't touch anything more than the face, shoulders, and arms. At the point when you're prepared to do as such, add a touch to the legs, back, and stomach to your interactions. Then proceed onward to doing full body massage, excluding the erogenous zones. The point is to have the option to appreciate how the giving and receiving of these touches feel and allowing you to appreciate the sensuality without the weight of the experience leading to sex. Be certain you are taking turns providing these touches to one another.

Attempt Safe and Fun Role Playing

When you feel progressively great with the above exercises, consider using pretending procedures to carry on coquettish scenes and jobs that are appealing and a good time for both of you. This can be a fun route for you and your accomplice to reproduce your first experience or make a new experience to serve further to increase want and sexual passion. Doing reverse pretends can serve to support you, and your accomplice perceives how one's interactions are interpreted by the other, which may likewise be useful in improving sexual intimacy with one another.

Discussing your Desires with your Partner

When discussing transforms, you might want to happen during sexual intimacy with your accomplice, be certain not to concentrate on the negatives by stating that everything you don't care for about them. Instead, center around the positive things you do like about them (sexual and non-sexual), then express a portion of the things you might want to witness, using phrases like "I might want it if____." Focusing on the positive viewpoints of your relationship intimacy rather than the negatives is an incredible method to increase want and sexual passion.

Chapter Three

ROMANCE

Many youthful couples assume that physical fascination is sufficient, yet we, as a whole, realize that it isn't sufficient. And we have to give more consideration to the main thing, building an unshakable establishment for breathtaking sex life, and everything that goes with it.

Two individuals who have demonstrated their adoration for one another and who have set up a unique association can mine the fortunes and savors the experience of the profundities of their feelings that others won't have the option to comprehend or reach. Accomplices who sincerely trust in one another and need to be together are going to encounter a multi-faceted intimacy that powers the most significant kind of association – one that happens in the body and soul! Not simply the body.

It's the sensitive inner feelings that issue. Nothing can replace feeling a certain exceptional shine for somebody. It's the little things that tally. At the point when you have an incredible enthusiastic association, you will normally identify with one another well in bed. So focus on both romance and connections when wooing that uncommon accomplice.

Think how much fun you and your mate can have in the event that you attempt a new, however entangled sex method in a cheerful manner, speedy to snicker at your very own ungainliness and bombed first endeavors, and allowing each other time to ace the system.

You would not flop by any stretch of the imagination. Simply trying something new is a triumph. And it will take some training to make it a smooth, commonly satisfying experience. As you learn, you will make some pleasant recollections and have a lot of snickers en route. And why not? Who said sex must be so darn genuine?

It is shrewd certainly and make a high level of solace for your accomplice and yourself, so you can examine your endeavors and offer your feelings in an undemanding climate, liberated from performance uneasiness!

If you approach it in a genuine-minded manner and anticipate flawlessness, or quick outcomes, while refusing to discuss it, you will sit idle, however, make more worry for your relationship, and both of you will wind up suffering peacefully.

Luckily, building an incredible sex life is a long voyage loaded with startling wanders aimlessly. The more you come to know and regard your mate, the more delight your relationship will have the option to sustain as time goes on. The more profoundly you will have the option to identify with one another sexually.

Anybody can have a medium-term fling. That isn't particularly satisfying, and the impacts are fleeting, though an extraordinarily intimate relationship can fill you with a significant fulfillment every way under the sun. Sex is only one of the preferences!

The individuals who need a brilliant and profoundly satisfying sex life - one that approaches joy - must form their château on an unshakable establishment of genuine love and intimacy. I won't dwell on the point, yet I feel constrained to pressure this basic truth for the individuals who need to hear it. Simply recollect romance and connections blend well.

And incredible sex occurs as a feature of an extraordinary life, wherein the two accomplices are continually learning and growing and experimenting. Each is flourishing in its own right — every life's existence of direction and passion. Actual existence is given to love and support, and not narrow-minded undertakings will be bound to help the demands of a remarkable sex life than some other.

That is another point that has a significant effect. Incredible sex originates from giving. Incredible darlings are extraordinary providers. They put their cherished first in the bedroom and spend their lives contributing in positive manners to the welfare and happiness of others.

In the event that you are childish and conceited, you won't make a decent darling to your accomplice. Happiness originates from pleasing you're adored. You won't appreciate an incredible sex life some other way. Hello, I didn't make up the rules. That is only the manner in which it is.

Romance Effect on Love and Relationships

Romance and Its Effect on Love and Relationships: The craving of each man and woman is to have a fulfilling relationship, and for your relationship to be satisfied, there must be a lot of romance in it. Romance is the ingredient that includes a pleasant landscape into a relationship. It makes a relationship progressively appealing. It generally continues adding something of uncommon essentialness to adore life.

Connections need romance to make an air of satisfaction. Having bliss in your relationship will bring the sparkling impacts of magnificence into your life. Couples must have the option to utilize romance viably in request to attain their objective of delight.

People consistently have something excellent in them, and they just open it to their cherished one, this disclosure is generally through romance. It additionally shows the excellence of your inner self. You need to show the outstanding character that has charmed every one of you to each other, and this can here, and there be accomplished by showing your romantic wants to each other. Opening up to one another is extremely wonderful in light of the fact that it enables your accomplice to know the individual that lives within you. They can understand how you think and why you carry on the manner in which you do. As both of you uncover inner contemplations, wants, shortcomings, and qualities, a more grounded bond creates. This is the thing that makes romance a wonderful pathway for couples to go on with their connections.

Romance Effect on Love and Relationships

The following Are Some Reasons Why Romance Makes Relationships so Beautiful:

1. IT BRINGS COUPLES TOGETHER –

It is the magnet that binds couples together through fascination. They will, in general, observe something exceptional in one another. They find extraordinary qualities that invigorate them to be pulled in to one another. Through romance, they find things that they both like and share for all intents and purposes.

2. IT REVEALS THEIR ZEAL FOR EACH OTHER –

It makes their relationship more beneficial in light of the fact that it brings out their exciting interests. With this, they will continue to investigate the marvels and experiences that go with having a satisfying relationship. They will continue to move and find things that they share practically speaking and enhance them. They will continue searching for things that they can do in a request to make their relationship increasingly energetic and meaningful.

3. IT WILL BRING OUT THEIR RE-SPECT FOR ONE ANOTHER –

Romance is so excellent on the grounds that it regards the necessities of each other.

They should be thought about

At the point when they regard each other, they exceptionally esteemed their relationship. Romantic Relationships that are wonderful in such a manner will never blur away.

An orgasm is a physical reflex, expedited through sexual incitement, most regularly that of the clitoris, which is the most delicate organ in the vagina. "It's a development to a time allotment during sexual incitement where there's simply this enormous arrival of joy.

During sexual excitement, the bloodstream increases to the private parts, and your muscles tense all through your body. The orgasm then "reverses this procedure through a progression of musical withdrawals. During an orgasm, "endorphins are discharged into the circulatory system, and these synthetics may make you feel cheerful, jubilant, flushed, warm, or drowsy."

Do I need to orgasm during sex?

This is a convoluted inquiry in light of the fact that, no, in fact, you don't need to orgasm during sex. Vaginal entrance or incitement can even now feel great without reaching a sexual peak. And organically speaking, regardless of whether you're trying to have an infant, a vaginal orgasm isn't essential (obviously, the penis must discharge since sperm is expected to treat the egg). That being stated, there might be a natural motivation behind why we have vaginal orgasms: with the goal that we need to engage in sexual relations again. "It bodes well that sex feels better with the goal that you are happy to have intercourse,

What are the types of orgasms?

Here's a list of the most well-known types of orgasms and what they commonly feel like, if this fluctuates from individual to individual:

Clitoral- - These orgasms are regularly felt on the outside of the body, similar to a tingly feeling along the skin and in your brain.

Vaginal- - These orgasms are more profound in the body and can without much of a stretch be felt by the individual penetrating the vagina in light of the fact that the vaginal dividers will beat.

Anal- - Before the huge O, you may feel an intense need to pee. However, the withdrawals definitely won't be searched for the privates. Instead, they'll be around the anal sphincter.

Combo- - When the vagina — particularly the G-spot — and the clitoris are animated simultaneously, it will work in general outcome in a progressively touchy motion picture style orgasm that may have to convulse or truly discharge (read: female discharge isn't a legend).

Erogenous zones- - Lesser-known parts of your body, for example, the ears, the areolas, the neck, the elbows, and the knees, can, in any case, cause a pleasurable response when kissed and played with. For increasingly delicate individuals, continuous play may prompt an orgasm.

Presently, how would we cause these orgasms to occur?

How about we talk about the clitoris

The clitoris is a little organ with a ton of nerve endings that looks out from the tiptop of the vulva, is regularly secured by a hood, and reaches out down the inside of the labia. The ideal approach to animate the clitoris is by delicately rubbing with the fingers, palm, or tongue in a to and fro or roundabout movement.

Clitoral orgasm

Once the clitoris begins to get wet — or after you include lube because not all vaginas can get wet without anyone else — apply quicker and harder weight in a redundant movement.

Tackling the slippery vaginal orgasm

Vaginal orgasm is frequently confused as the "best" route for ladies to orgasm (read: the simplest for penises). However, it's regularly the hardest for women. Instead of a penis, attempt fingers or a sex toy. Insert the fingers or toy into the vagina and make a "come hither" movement toward the paunch button.

There's a point of delight on this divider called the G-spot, and when you hit it with standard, solid weight, it can prompt orgasm. The incitement of the G-spot is additionally the best approach to prompt female discharge, as it animates the Skene's glands on either side of the urethra.

Vaginal orgasm

Aim to utilize fingers or a toy for infiltration instead of the penis.

Anal orgasm

Anal orgasms are considerably more typical in men as a result of the prostate, yet can likewise be accomplished essentially by rubbing the outside of the anal opening just as stimulating the inside of the butt with a finger. With regards to anal sex, it would be ideal if you, if it's not too much trouble, please use lube. Butts don't normally deliver oil, and the skin around the region is inclined to tears, which can prompt undesirable infection.

Shop for grease online.

In case you're looking to give back in kind with your male partner, invigorate the prostate by delicately inserting a finger straight forward and massage the gland.

The combo and erogenous orgasm

In request to accomplish a combo orgasm, combine clitoral and vaginal incitement simultaneously, either in parallel or inverse rhythms — whatever feels best for you or your partner. This is likewise the most well-known approach to accomplish female discharge on the grounds that the clitoris is invigorated, and the G-spot or Skene's glands are locked in.

Finally, erogenous zone orgasms are accomplished only through a great deal of experimentation. You might have the option to orgasm from kisses on your neck, teeth on your areolas, or fingers on the inside of your elbows. The ideal approach to find your erogenous zones is to utilize a feather or another light outside the item and observe where you feel the most joy.

Orgasms won't come without correspondence.

In any kind of sexual play, openness is absolutely vital. Not exclusively is assent actually legally necessary, however telling your partner what you need, how, and where is the ideal approach to guarantee the greatest delight. It's optimal to have these discussions before engaging in sexual play. However, it's similarly viable to control your partner during sex. This implies asking for what you need, either with words or with your body language. Keep in mind, partners aren't minded per users, despite the fact that we need them to be.

This likewise implies being available to experimentation. In the event that your customary sex routine isn't getting you off, then experimenting with touching new regions on various occasions with various body parts (private parts, fingers, and mouths) is the following best advance to solving your orgasm riddle.

It's essential to take note of that experimenting and achieving orgasm doesn't require a partner. Joy isn't needy, and neither are you — the better you know your mood with fingers and toys, the quicker you can show your partner how you tango.

What really occurs during an orgasm.

What physically occurs in a woman's body during genuine orgasm is this: the vagina, uterus, and rear-end (and now and again other body parts like hands, feet, and guts) contract quickly, squeezing for 0.8 seconds one after another. Ladies may likewise discharge, releasing a fluid out of the urethra that contains a blend of whitish liquid from the Skene'speri-urethral glands and urine. Try not to stress — urine is extremely sterile, and the fluid, for the most part, turns out clear.

In any case, not everybody encounters sex and orgasm in a similar way. The above clarifications are incredible starting points. However, sex doesn't have a manual. That is the reason for exploring in the minute, and finding what your body adores is totally key.

Understanding the phases that lead to orgasm may support you

Experts and Johnson composed a book that point by point, the sexual reaction cycle, which expresses that there are four phases of the sexual reaction:

Chapter Four

ADVICES

- Excitement. Initially being turned on.

- Plateau. A tedious movement that feels pleasurable.

- Orgasm. The explosion of joy and discharge.

- Resolution. The refractory time frame.

While this is, for the most part, precise, it's too broad — particularly when these stages traverse, and there are no dangerous goals. It's additionally inaccurate to recommend that sex finishes in orgasm since this prevents many ladies from claiming their orgasms by pushing that sex are finished when their male partners finish. Furthermore, not all sex requires an orgasm, and orgasms don't mean the sex is extraordinary.

Orgasms can be little. They can happen many occasions in succession or just once, and they don't generally occur. Try not to define your orgasms by another person's depiction... that is, at last, shorting yourself on delight. Your quiet clitoral orgasm can, in any case, be mind-blowing, similarly as your combo orgasm can be fun, and your partner's discharge can be exciting.

Bodies are unique. Orgasms are unique. Be that as it may, the way it takes to arrive is tied in with experimenting, communicating, and trying again. Enable yourself to absorb the impressions of the delight procedure the same amount of, or considerably more than, the finale.

Foreplay has a notoriety for being a warm-up or leads into sex, and the hors d'oeuvre to the main course—which is intercourse. Yet, perhaps it's time we stop thinking about it in such an old-school way. All things considered, just 30% of ladies can arrive at orgasm from penis-in-vagina entrance alone. It's the moves we ordinarily think of as foreplay—clitoral stroking, profound kissing, and oral sex—that bring most ladies to the statures of delight.

Touching tongues gets me stirred instantly.'

It's straightforward, yet it works unfailingly, and touching tongues gets me stirred instantly. If there are a little neck and ear biting and licking added to the blend, which is amazing, too. At the point when my partner and I take part in this kind of foreplay for significant stretches, it gets me truly energized for sex; the expectation factor develops my excitement and his, too. It can, in some cases, be significantly more pleasurable than the entrance itself."

'Areola activity makes me insane in an ideal manner.'

I like it, when my partner sucks on my areolas—nothing too hard, however when I'm as of now turned on a bit, it feels like the sensation is multiplied. It makes me insane, however, in an ideal manner."

Foreplay, the imperative entr'acte to intercourse, is the best warm-up of all the warm-ups. You run a little before you race to warm up. It's fine, yet it doesn't heat up your accomplice for sex. You do some air squats before your Cross fit WOD. That may fire up your muscles, yet it won't put your better half on the precarious edge of climax. You warm up your fire cook before you hurl the steak on. It gives the meat a charming consume, in any case, that sizzle is only half as alluring as her staggering breathing after some significant petting. Foreplay gets her there.

The scouring, contacting, kissing, and talking before sex that is foreplay is as basic to extraordinary sex as certified intercourse itself. It relaxes up both of you, gets you in the aura, bolsters your drives, and jump-starts the system to the basic erogenous zones that light up already and during sex. Do it right, and you'll prime your accomplice for an extraordinary climax. Hence, like a light run is incorporated into your run or warming up the fire sear is a piece of the cooking strategy, foreplay ought to be a coordinated piece of your sexual coexistence. That is the explanation we moved toward sex and relationship experts for their best admonishment and foreplay tips for making a huge segment of possibly the most critical piece of sex. Sex advisors and authorities offered their foreplay information that helps women with getting turned on for sex, and bring you closer at the same time. Endeavor one, or two, or the total of the foreplay tips underneath at whatever point you start playing around. The time spent concentrating on her body and feeling before entrance conveys benefits in her pleasure, and yours, when the enormous last act happens.

Foreplay Tips to Please Her in Bed

1) Sext for the duration of the day

Foreplay doesn't just begin in the bedroom. It can begin from the minute you wake up. Little messages like "Can hardly wait to get exposed with you tonight" can get your partner energized before you even set foot in a similar room. If sending nude pictures is something that turns and stirs your partner on, feel free to swap some sexy photos with each other. Then you can content what you need and plan to do to her bare body.

2) Take your time removing vestments

Foreplay is a long-distance race, not a sprint. You're in no rush to finish it. (Even though on the off chance that you are in a hurry, here are the best sex position for quick ones.) Instead of rapidly stripping down, start by taking off her shirt. Hold on for some moments before you remove her jeans, then her bra, and so on. You would then be able to concentrate on that newly uncovered body part. So in the wake of taking off her jeans, massage her legs. When the bra is gone, you can lick and tenderly suck on her areolas.

3) Give her a strip bother

In a comparable vein, feel free to give her a little strip bother. If you move inadequately, in any event, you put on a show of being endearing and entertaining, yet on the off chance that you do in truth strip well, she will need to jump on you.

4) Wear sexy clothing

Sexy underpants aren't only for ladies. If you find the correct fit, you can truly turn her on. (On the off chance that you've never attempted low-ascent briefs, we enthusiastically prescribe them!)

5) The precoital massage

As a warmup to the main occasion, start by massaging the length of her legs, from her upper thighs down to her lower legs.

Next, center around the feet, kneading her impact points and every single other point underneath. Then focus on the toes and stretch them individually — extra points on the off chance that you finish it off by sucking on them.

6) Ask what turns her on

If all else fails, simply come right out and ask what she loves during sex. "Most ladies acknowledge men who need to ensure they're fulfilled. If she sees you're working hard to satisfy her, she'll be bound to give back.

7) Focus on quality, not the amount

Improve the nature of foreplay, and she'll never again bug you about the amount. "If you go about as though you're simply going through the movements to get to the sex, she will notice, and it will take more time for her to get energized.

In other words, would what you like to do, and appreciate it while you're doing it on the off chance that you like how her calves feel, stroke them in appreciation. If you like her butt, kiss it. "At the point when a man is loving what he's doing, it will show through and turn her on, too.

8) Take it simple from the start

Truly, the clitoris is the conspicuous spot to concentrate — many men foul-up by it. "Direct incitement of the clitoris can be painful. "It's vastly improved to rub the clitoral hood [where the tops of the labia meet] or to rub at the edge of the clitoris than it is to go straight for its head."

If you are playing with the clitoris during oral sex, it is recommended to "center on the clitoris, then don't concentrate on the clitoris."

The clitoris responds best to being prodded, so you need to lick it and suck on it a bit, construct somewhat strain, then back off on it a piece before going at it again.

9) Expand your repertoire

There are a lot of approaches to expand your oral sex repertoire, and you ought to consistently be looking to include new moves and blend things up. First of all, trying lying opposite to her body and stroking her clitoris with your tongue in an even movement, rather than all over. She'll welcome the adjustment in incitement, ideally enough to give back.

10) Drive her wild with the figure-8 procedure

The figure-8 tongue procedure is one of the most proven approaches to get things moving underhanded. At the point when you're at her administration down beneath, work the supersensitive region around her clitoris in a figure-8 example. Stimulate her with delicate sucking until the little button swells, then cautiously uncover the zone with your fingers.

Utilize the tricky underside of your tongue to hover it to one side and then to one side. With the more unpleasant top side of the tongue, flick from right to left and then here and there.

11) Don't disregard the labia

Oft disregarded as unimportant obstructions to the vagina, the labia are pressed with nerve endings and shouldn't be overlooked. Hold every one between your thumb and forefinger and massage it, working your way here and there.

Or, on the other hand, using the entirety of your fingers and your palm, "smoosh" the labia together, practically like you're (tenderly!) kneading batter.

12) Explore her whole body

Don't only focus on her privates. The body is loaded up with erogenous zones like her neck, thighs, and bosoms.

"Privates are fascinating and fun, yet attempt to invest some energy focusing on your partner's whole body instead of going straight for her groin. "Have a go at caressing, licking, or nibbling other erogenous zones, for example, her neck, back, ears, a midsection.

13) Try a sex toy

A vibrator sex toy buzzing around her erogenous zones can be similarly as stimulating, if not more, than your hands alone. Bring one in for the help during foreplay, touching her all over; however, her vagina with it.

14) Don't go on and on

Be cautious about what you state when you're trying to set the disposition and construct excitement.

"Odd, worn-out expressions can make the state of mind bite the dust rapidly. When in doubt, keep messy talk straightforward and individual: Pick a body part and disclose to her how sexy it is, or depict a dream you have involving her."

Then again, don't shut your mouth altogether. "Ladies need mental incitement.

15) Pay consideration regarding how she feels

Everybody is unique, so ensure you're ready to peruse how she reacts to what you're doing. It shouldn't be difficult to determine what's working and to utilize this information then to prop something worth being thankful for up.

"On the off chance that she winces when you speak profanely, move onto your next play, "Or if she's truly into making out on the couch, don't attempt to move it to the bedroom."

16) Pay consideration regarding how you feel

In case you're stressed over getting off too right on time during intercourse, take a stab at becoming increasingly mindful of your pre-orgasmic sensations.

Most men just perceive that last, no-turning-back feeling, that happens just before discharge. By then it's too late to take care of business.

Attempt to get comfortable with the few increasingly unpretentious vibes that go before that one, so you can back off at the opportune time.

17) Don't disregard kissing

Ladies get their most prominent sexual delight from the visit, passionate kissing. On the off chance that you get the feeling that she's starting to lose interest, kissing is consistently the ideal approach to bring her to go into it."

Simply recall that passionate kissing doesn't constantly mean wildly swabbing out her tonsils. Attempt to stir up your tongue play with the incidental shut mouth kiss on her nose, eyes, and forehead.

18) Reward her valiance

At the point when she initiates the activity, endeavor to satisfy her sexually and to tell her how much you endorse. Disclose to her; you cherished how she got things moving. Some of the time, ladies wonder in case you're going to see initiation as negative or on the off chance that it may make you awkward.

19) Know when to skip it

On the off chance that you as of now have great sexual science, it's splendidly OK to skip foreplay incidentally.

At the point when you've been creating a bigger sexual setting in your relationship, you're fundamentally operating in that [state of foreplay] constantly. "If you've been together for some time, you should realize her alright to realize when it's alright to bounce directly to the main occasion.

Cunnilingus is a type of oral sex, with which the clitoris and the vulva are animated via caressing the tongue. In an exacting interpretation, the word cunnus is deciphered from Latin, similar to female genital organs, and the word lingo signifies "licking."

Kinds of cunnilingus

There are a few kinds of strokes, which in the cutting edge world is known as the word cunnilingus. The most well-known interpretation, which includes such activities as licking, sucking, and kissing intimate organs. Once in a while, here likewise include light biting of the clitoris. Various strategies of cunnilingus involve varieties. Now and again, it's developments in the tongue in the vagina, which recreate contacts, and you can likewise stroke the accessible regions with your nose. Sometimes, cunnilingus is joined by erosion, performed with the fingers. There is additionally a rather colorful type of oral sex when strokes are performed by the chin, yet this isn't to everybody's liking since even a crisply shaven male chin is still somewhat thorny. In some cases, cunnilingus utilizes sexual toys to invigorate the remainder of the erogenous zones more adequately than with just hands or tongue.

How cunnilingus is done

Before you continue, you should deal with that the woman was in an agreeable position. On the off chance that she cannot appropriately unwind, she won't arrive at the phase of excitation fundamental for orgasm. The best part is that if she lies on her back, you can likewise put a pad under her hips, so you would be progressively agreeable. Cautiously "open" the hands of the outside genitalia, with the goal that the clitoris is noticeable all around. To begin caressing is best with a light and fast touch of the tongue along the vulva. Slow and overwhelming licking - not the most suggestive stroke, although you should attempt various choices since everybody feels it suddenly. Slowly you can begin to move toward the region of the clitoris. Turn your tongue around him, then you can begin on occasion effectively and rapidly grabbing him, and at exactly that point, continue straightforwardly to the touches of this very body. Try not to stroke the clitoris continuously; Otherwise, joy will rapidly be supplanted by bothering or even pain. Frequently cunnilingus is diminished to incitement of the clitoris, as this is the most touchy organ, yet this procedure requires uncommon propriety. In the beginning periods of touching, it tends to be painful, regardless of whether they are done delicately and with language. For this situation, it is smarter, to begin with licking the surrounding territories, bit by bit getting near the clitoris, so he could get energized. If you don't need your partner to get an orgasm too immediately, then remember to be occupied and focus on the erogenous zones around the clitoris. You can likewise touch everything you can reach. Cunnilingus is an incredible method to animate, in which you can get both a fast orgasm and a moderate one, and the sub-sequent one contrasts inside and out and more extensive scope of sensations. Signs that you are bending the stick or have begun something too early: the partner involuntarily flinches and attempts to move away from your mouth. For this situation, it is important to make strokes progressively delicate and simpler, paying more consideration regarding the vulva.

Here, a few tips for going down on your woman as well as anyone:

1. It will be ideal if you stop pointing your tongue

She should consistently be on edge to gain and get comprehension and data, be freed from eagerness, and consistently have a preference for get-togethers, and for human expressions.

Coming up next are the standard characteristics of all things considered:

"Most ladies don't care for a pointy, hard tongue on the clit. "Have a go at flattening your tongue and using general terms."

Rehash after me: general terms. General terms. The hard, jabbing tip of your mouth-muscle is giving nobody an orgasm at any point shortly.

2. Feel free to utilize your hands

Most cunnilingus-suppliers aren't reluctant to push a finger or two up in there while going down, which is extraordinary. Tribby proposes curling two fingers up towards her tummy button once they're inserted, and using a "firm 'come hither' movement" to invigorate the g-spot.

Yet! Fingering her isn't the best way to incorporate your hands.

"You can likewise utilize the labia to massage the clit by delicately pressing the lips together and kneading the clit between your fingers. "Putting firm weight on the mons pubis (the hill) and incorporating roundabout movements will likewise conscious the nerves."

3. To toy or not to toy (to toy!)

There's confusion (I trust it's a misinterpretation, in any case) that men out there are intimidated by sex toys. Nothing can supplant a genuine, human dick don't as well, stress. In any case, that doesn't mean a decent toy can't help with oral, particularly because – well, you most likely can't get your dick up there simultaneously, and in some cases, it's pleasant to have an entrance that doesn't involve a fingernail.

Most famous toy among the Pleasure Chest staff is the Pjur Wand since it's "impeccably intended for accessing the G-Spot..it's additionally slim enough to avoid your mouth's way."

4. Continue through to the end, a.k.a. focus

There's nothing more awful than when your partner has discovered an extremely super-mood with you; they're licking endlessly, and then abruptly, they choose that since you're so into it, they should begin going as quick and hard as humanly conceivable exactly when you're going to come.

Instead, in case you're doing something that has your woman writhing with delight, simply fucking continue doing it. You will know she's writhing with delight by the way that she is writhing. In request to see that, however, you'll need to escape your head (ha) and spotlight on her developments.

Regularly, when ladies need more, they will push their hips towards your mouth. "When you found the development that works, reiteration is critical.

5. Disregard what you realized in secondary school

If what you realized in secondary school is that forming the letters A-Z with your tongue is the best approach to make a woman come, I lament to disclose to you that you've been woefully misinformed.

"A major misinterpretation is that individuals ought to compose the letter set with their tongue. This is senseless because when you're concentrating on letters in your head, you're not paying thoughtfulness regarding her sign in the occasion."

Tribby proposes creating suction around the clit, as though it were the head of a penis and continually using a level tongue to go to and fro.

Keep these rules handy, and you will have a glad woman on your hands. And in your mouth (COULD NOT RESIST).

Chapter Five

FELLATIO

Whether you utilize the specialized term fellatio or consider it a blowjob, going down, giving head, or something else, performing fellatio is a demonstration that requires a great deal of trust and a smidgen of information.

In the event that you think everything you hear, you may think that folks love this so much strategy and intent don't make a difference. Think again. In actuality, there is a great deal of variety in fellatio abilities, and knowing how to peruse your partner, what to do to him, and when to do it can have a significant effect.

We, for the most part, think of fellatio as being one individual licking or sucking a partner's penis. Remember that while most men have penises, not all do. And not every person who has a penis consistently needs to or can utilize it for sexual joy. So this article centers around just a single method for performing oral sex on a man.

How to Perform Fellatio

Start off Nice and Clean

Social disgrace appears to concentrate on the flavor of ladies' private parts more than men's. Men can smell and taste similarly as solid as ladies. In case you're new to fellatio, you may be stressed over taste and smell. Assuming this is the case, recommend a sexy shower or shower together and start with a fresh start. While the counterfeit tastes might be no better (and can be a lot of more awful), a few people like to utilize enhanced oil or put on a seasoned condom, which may not taste better yet accompanies the additional advantage of making oral sex somewhat more secure.

Physical Comfort Is Key

You can't have a ton of fun and perform well in case you're not physically agreeable, and fellatio may put a strain on your neck & jaw. Kneeling before your partner on a cushion, while he's standing or sitting, gives you a decent scope of movement and a lot of access. If you've had awful encounters with fellatio where you felt the absence of control, have him on his back and hunch in the middle of his legs. Giving head can place you in a significant power position on the off chance that you like that feeling, then pull out all the stops.

Bother With Touch

Using your hands first, delicately stroked his inner thighs, penis, scrotum, gonads, and perineum, paying regard for his responses (verbal and facial) as you touch certain spots. Many men who have affectability in their penis are particularly touchy around the head (known as the glans), particularly the frenulum, an indentation between the glans and the pole on the underside of the penis. You should brush up on your insight into male sexual anatomy, to comprehend what you're working with.

Give Him a Lick

Catch up with your tongue, exploring a similar terrain using moderate wide strokes with your tongue. Try not to be hesitant to utilize heaps of spit, as this common lube feels extraordinary and makes contact and suction. Many sexually transmitted infections can be passed during fellatio; using seasoned condoms is an incredible method to rehearse more secure sex and manage any taste you dislike. It is additionally one approach to help folks who state they experience issues with condoms become accustomed to, and amped up for, using them.

Take Him in Your Mouth

At the point when he's semi-erect, gradually manage your lips over the tip of his penis, making sure your lips spread your teeth as you slide delicately down his pole similarly as you're agreeable. Keep your mouth rigid, as the weight from your lips will feel extraordinary as they skim down the penis. Put him in your mouth before he is completely erect is a decent method for getting settled with the size of his penis, particularly on the off chance that he is in the bigger range.

Watch Your Gag Reflex

In case you're not proficient at the profound throat (taking the entire penis in your mouth), trying to do it without practicing first will probably trigger your stifler reflex. It's redundant, and a comparative impact can be accomplished with the hand and mouth procedure portrayed beneath. With training, you can figure out how to loosen up your muffle reflex and take in a greater amount of the penis.

Utilize Your Mouth and Tongue

As your head goes up the underside of the penis, straighten your tongue, so it gives the frenulum a pleasant wide, wet stroke. Try to attempt various sorts of licks or kisses—the lips feel great when flown over the edge of the penis—however, play out each stroke more than once before changing to give predictable delight.

Play around With the Foreskin

If your partner is uncircumcised, insert your tongue into the foreskin and hover around the head with it. You can likewise utilize your fingers to tenderly massage the head through the foreskin, alternating with profound tongue licks.

Using Your Mouth and Hand, Tip #1

An incredible blowjob isn't just about a month and a penis. Spot one hand around the pole of his penis while you go all over on the top portion of his penis. Have a go at coordinating your developments, so your hand and mouth are going here and there as one. On the off chance that your partner is thrusting, your hand will keep his penis from being pushed too far into your mouth.

Using Your Mouth and Hand

On the off chance that he prefers this combination, bring your hand as far as possible up the pole (following your mouth), evacuate your mouth quickly, utilize your palm to slide and contort over the head (as though you were juicing an orange), and then float your hand down pursued by your mouth again. Rehash.

Allow Him to come

At the point when he's prepared to orgasm, keep your developments steady and firm — don't relax. When he begins ejaculating, oversee him with a couple of strokes and then stop, as most men don't need continued incitement once they've discharged and had an orgasm.

To Swallow or Not to Swallow?

This choice is completely up to you. There's nothing amiss with you on the off chance that you would prefer not to, yet it's pleasant to tell your partner it's nothing close to home. If you would prefer not to swallow, and you aren't acquainted with the indications of imminent discharge, let him realize you need a warning. Expel your mouth as he's going to discharge, and continue hand stroking through his orgasm.

Tips

1. Don't overlook the remainder of his body. The scrotum and gonads (balls) are particularly delicate, and most men like them to be animated.

Attempt gently licking or touching his balls during oral sex. He may likewise like them to be supported tenderly in one of your hands. A few men go wild when you place your hand around the top of the scrotum and delicately pull down.

2. You can likewise apply strain to his perineum (the spot between his butt and his penis) with a couple of fingers, as this additionally can feel better.

3. He may like wearing a butt plug or other toy during fellatio for included prostate incitement. Or on the other hand, you can apply strain to his butt with one of your fingers.

Fellatio Sex Positions

The well-known axiom used to go; the path to a man's heart is through his stomach... an entirely decent tip if you have a talent for the k itchen... For the individuals who don't, or plan on launching a two-dimensional assault for their man, learning the fellatio group of sex positions is an incredible spot to begin...

Supported Cock Sex Position

Otherwise known as His 68

Offering incredible access for analingus, tea bagging, and fellatio, the Cradled Cock takes treating a man to the following level... particularly on the off chance that she brings him a cushion for his head. She would almost certainly profit by having various cushions herself to lessen the strain of keeping raised. We likewise prescribe for men to disseminate, however much of their weight as could reasonably be expected between their feet and shoulders since she likely won't value having somebody sitting on her bosoms.

Fuck Face Sex Position

Otherwise known as Face Fuck

Featuring one of the less proper names in our rundown, Fuck Face is a top fan choice. A moderately straight forward position, there isn't too a lot to the state beyond it being possibly somewhat hard for ladies to have the option to stroke with their hands while resting on their elbows. It can likewise be a touch of straining on a woman's neck, so we prescribe to try different things with kneeling at various statures to find the most agreeable position.

Plumber Sex Position

Earning its name from its likeness to a Plumber getting under the sink, this position is a very agreeable path for ladies to heat the channel.

With the man kneeling on every one of the fours, ladies have incredible access for some tushy and gonad time, just as exploring a few streets less voyaged, however, it's most likely a smart thought to thump before getting named as a trespasser. There is, however, a little drawback, or rather a shallow one, as the arrangement of her mouth and throat are not perfect for profound throating.

Stand and Blow Sex Positio

Otherwise known as Atten-Hut

The Stand and Blow position may be the ideal approach to respect a man's home. However, that doesn't mean one needs to trust that their man will leave and come back to perform it. Requiring no furnishings and next to no space, it is adaptable in where it very well may be performed, and one of minimal straining on a woman's neck. The main drawback is that it could be somewhat tough on her knees when done on a hard floor, so think about throwing a few pads down to include a little solace.

Sword Swallower Sex Position

Otherwise known as Throat Swab

A 180 bend on Tea Bag, the Sword Swallower position has the man facing towards his partner. On account of the almost straight arrangement of the woman's mouth and throat, it will, in general, be truly outstanding for profound throating and happens to be very agreeable too. On the off chance that that wasn't sufficient motivation to look at it, it is likewise the best in the class for viewing and playing with her bosoms! Given how troublesome it tends to be to breathe while profound throating, we energetically prescribe for anybody new to the game to begin moderate. Since verbal correspondence can be somewhat tough with a significant piece, ladies should put their hands on the man's hips to manage speed, profundity, and in particular, air breaks.

Open Usual Sex Position

The Open Usual is an inconspicuous variety of The Usual, where the man spreads his legs open, and the woman lies between them. Albeit a little distinction on paper, this has a colossal effect on the measure of gonad and anal play that is conceivable. It's a smart thought to have a few pads under the man's back to tilt his pelvis and improve the entrance considerably more.

Contorted Usual Sex Position

The Usual with a Twist and, additionally, the grounded type of Oral Therapy, the Twisted Usual, is the best thing a man could wake up to. Offering ladies somewhat more versatility over The Usual, the key distinction is that the closer position of her body puts her within his compass, allowing for an assortment of strategies to restore some delight. We prescribe for men to spread their legs a little to give their partner better access to wherever else the sun doesn't shine and think about certain pads under the man's back to alter tallness and to lessen neck strain.

Tea Bag Sex Position

A 180 bend on the Sword Swallower, the Tea Bag position has the man facing ceaselessly from his partner. Named for its unparalleled oral access to the gonads, it is additionally extraordinary for analingus. However, fellatio will probably require a free hand to help keep an erection pointed downwards. It tends to be exceptionally hard to perform when statures are skewed, so if your bed isn't working out so well, try to try different things with some other furniture to check whether you can find a superior fit and use cushions for fine-tuning.

Sit and Blow Sex Position

The Sit and Blow is an extraordinary method to make any man feel like the king of the palace... and we'd prefer to think that it was Bill's preferred method to get some empty talk in the oval. Easy to get into, and very agreeable, about the main thing we can truly say other than making more jokes is that a few pads on the floor are constantly a keen play when kneeling.

Certain beds accompany certain difficulties. A futon, for instance, is hard AF and gives you stature to work with, also the way that you're then stuck sleeping on a futon. Can't do much about that last thing, yet here's how to make the best out of any sleeping sitch.

1. in a Twin Bed: The Side Car

Twist-up on your side in the fetal position. Have your partner kneel on one leg by your sweet ass, while the other foot goes up by your knees for influence. On the off chance that he slides a well-lubed hand between your legs as he pushes, keep him around.

2. on a Futon: The Presser

Exploit the low stature by sitting with your butt at the very edge and leaning back on your hands.

Your partner kneels to enter, with his knees spread wide. He clutches your thighs to pull you still further onto him. The futon's supernatural solidness that infections you, when you're trying to rest, is your companion here. You get the deepest of the entrance, and in addition to on the off chance that you rub yourself with a hand, you'll will never again think about the entire futon thing.

3. in a Sleeping Bag: The Top CAT

Odds are in case you're in a sleeping sack with him; you're into him. Make your association closer with a variety of the moderate romantic grind that is the Coital Alignment Technique (CAT). You rest on top of him and slide your body down his until the top portion of his penis is rubbing against your vulva/clit district. Grind, rub, and slide yourself over his penis—the development is all going to be in your hips. Be that as it may, here's the best piece: the moderate form and clit-centered incitement exponentially help your chances of having an orgasm.

4. In a Loft: The Loft Slide

In space, you've got to remain low—however, this is nothing yet uplifting news for fanatics of grinding. The key here is your partner's leg between your legs so you can press against their thigh (feel free to lube it up). In case you're with a person, ensure there's sufficient of an edge so their penis won't sever. In case you're with a woman, and you need to include something extra, she can wear a lash on, or you can writhe against her. For either set of gear, it's anything but difficult to add a toy or hand to the merriments.

5. In a Bottom Bunk: Electric 69

There's very little stature, very little width—so get inventive with a 69 crossbreed. Lie on your sides, yet instead of your partner using their mouth on you, hand them an amazing toy. If it's a penis that is in your face, utilize your mouth or a masturbation sleeve. On the off chance that it's a V you're dealing with, respond with their preferred toy. The best part: In a standard 69, when a partner gets too turned on, their mouth simply kind of... decreases... however, a toy just continues chugging along.

Chapter Six

CLASSIC POSITIONS

Oral on Demand

While both are giving and receiving oral sex are a portion of our preferred approaches to arrive at the peak, the main disadvantage is, well, normally, you need another individual present. This progression with the ORA™ 2, an oral sex simulator that gives you the impression of superior to genuine oral sex in a toy that resembles nothing you've at any point seen previously. It's ideal for lying back on a heap of cushions or in your bath to indulge in oral delight that leaves nobody with an irritated jaw... well, perhaps you from moaning. Liquefy into an oral obsession with a snapshot of genuine euphoria.

Stand Up for Stand out Pleasure

For the appeal of waterproof sex toys, we don't hear much about ladies standing up when they jerk off, however, the opportunity has already come and gone that changes! An additional advantage, either with your foot against the divider as you lean in reverse or upon a stool or the side of your tub as you stand unassisted, this position lets you put that additional weight that you may want for an extra intense sensation. There are a ton of G-spot vibrators that are extraordinary for this position, both for outer clitoral or internal joy. One of our preferred approaches to utilize them is really when standing and leaning forward against a divider with our bowed knee squeezed against the divider (with the foot resting on a low stool), so you can push against the massager to more readily hit the G-spot.

Rocker and Roller

In a general public where man-spreading spins out of control and unchallenged, here and there, you simply want to set yourself up in a major, boss seat, and letting yourself feel like a total chief. At the point when you're craving this certainty, we have a performance sex position for you which you can use in an assortment of ways, as on the couch while watching Fifty Shades of Gray, in your home office seat fantasizing about a work romance, or in one of our top picks: a huge rocking seat — matched with the SIRI™ 2 handheld massager, which has a music-actuated massaging mode that is ideal for putting on a sex playlist and getting down at your party.

BETTY ROCKER POSITION

The Betty Rocker sex position is one that most couples never at any point attempt. It might look somewhat 'out there' or extraordinary, yet it's extremely simple to perform.

Your man needs to lie level on the bed with his legs only somewhat apart. You then need to straddle him, however instead of facing him, pivot, with the goal that he is presently looking at your back. While upstanding, slide his penis inside you, so you are currently in the Asian Cowgirl position with him. When he is inside you, begin to lean advances gradually and rest part of your weight on your arms or his legs.

LUNGE SEX POSITION

The Lunge sex position gets its name from the way that you will lunge on top of your man while performing it. This implies you have to have a smidgen of adaptability and quality if you need to play out the Lunge for a long length with your man. Some consider the To be as one of the oddity sex position, while others consider it to be an ordinary sex position.

To get into the Lunge position, your man needs to rests on the bed on his back, and he needs to open his legs. You are then going to get into a lunging position on top of him. To do this, start off by standing up straight on the bed, facing your man with your feet together just beneath his groin with your feet inside his legs.

IRISH GARDEN SEX POSITION

The Irish Garden is a fascinating sex position. At the point when a lot of couples see it first, they think that it requires an insane measure of adaptability. In all actuality, it doesn't. It's extremely simple to do. Here and there, the Irish Garden is very like the Betty Rocker position.

To get into the Irish Garden position, your man needs first to plunk down on the bed. He ought to have his back upstanding and straight. His legs ought to be out before him and opened genuinely wide. He can twist his knees on the off chance that it makes it increasingly agreeable for him. You then need to get down on every one of the fours and reverse yourself towards him. You will have let your abdomen down onto your man by straightening out your legs behind him (one on either side of his midsection). Presently lower your head and shoulders onto the bed until they are resting on it.

REVERSE COWGIRL POSITION

The Reverse Cowgirl sex position is one of the more outstanding sex positions out there. It's extraordinary for the individuals who like being on top of their man, yet would prefer not to invest all your energy looking into his eyes.

Getting into the Reverse Cowgirl position is simple and fortunately doesn't require a tremendous measure of adaptability. Your man first needs to begin by lying down on his back. You then need to get onto your knees, with one on either side of him, over his lap, so he is facing your back. Then simply drop yourself down on him.

Ordinary penetrative thrusting is great in a wide range of ways. Now is the right time tried, and feels dependably useful for the vast majority. Be that as it may, you can make your partner last longer (in addition to up your orgasmic potential) on the off chance that you move beyond the old in and out. Here's how.

1. The Knocker Rocker

Lie on your sides facing one another. Fold your upper leg and arm over your partner and rock him to and fro. This makes the incitement somewhat less intense for him, in addition to you get the chance to control the mood. He's responsible for playing with your boobs and assisting you with your preferred vibrator. Too intimate and feels amazing.

2. Missionary Impossible

If you hunger for a customary preacher involvement in the entirety of the eye-staring and whatnot, feel free to do it. Simply utilize a thicker condom (search for words like "additional quality" or "broadened joy") and utilize a grinding movement instead of a push. If he's as yet finishing too rapidly (as a result of the sheer intensity of your sexiness, natch), attempt a condom with a numbing ointment like benzocaine inside. Simply be careful about mouth-stuff a while later because that stuff truly numbs you up.

3. The Ball Monitor

You kneel over his lap facing his feet. Grind, rub, and push; however, you see fit. At the point when it appears as though he's going to orgasm, delicately pull on his balls, pulling them away from his body somewhat. (Tenderly!!) Repeat the succession long as you all can take it.

4. The Measuring Spoons

You're the inner spoon, and he's external. Open your legs wide and wrap your top leg back around his legs/butt to pull him closer. The thrusting movement tells a buddy's brain and/or a penis that he ought to have an orgasm immediately, so check them all out banging. Attempt a cadence of, state, eight shallow pushes to one profound hard one, with him thrusting in and up. He can amplify the moderate consume by cupping your vag with a well-lubed hand as he moves.

5. Dog, Interrupted

Switching positions fills in as a reset button on Masters and Johnson's phases to the peak. A decent method to change without a body part slipping out and everybody getting surly are starting in each of the positions of the four with your knees spread wide. At the point when he feels himself getting close, he sits out of sorts, pulling you somewhere around your hips onto his lap. Utilize the chance to touch yourself, him to chill off, and to begin back up again in an overly sexy position that hits quite a few spots.

Pregnancy Sex Positions That Are Absolute Fire

How does that familiar axiom go? "Pizza is a great deal like sex: When it's great, it's great. And when it's terrible... it's still truly great." OK, that is most likely valid for pizza, yet there's simply no reason for awful sex — regardless of whether you're pregnant.

It might pause for a moment to find your score during your pregnancy, yet what better time to try?

In case you're wringing your hands about whether pregnant sex is protected, don't pressure. A few couples will, in general, stress that intercourse could hurt or even rush their child directly out. Probably not. Counterfeit news. Try not to let these janky old fantasies take your O.

Pregnant sex is protected from appreciating (except for high-chance pregnancy factors like placenta previa), and it's useful for the momma-to-be and her partner.

For whatever length of time that you're physically agreeable, nearly everything is on the table. Along these lines, except if your doctor has given you the red light for reasons unknown, you reserve each privilege to get occupied.

Fortunate for you, we've gathered the best positions for getting jiggy during your pregnancy.

1. Jump on top

Indeed, you're the Christmas tree topper, and you're the shining star. In this manager move, you're in control, all things considered, — pace, point, and so forth. In the interim, your partner gets the full 5-star perspective on your excellent self.

This one is constantly a go-to, yet while pregnant, you may find that your body is more delicate than expected. Being on top methods, you're operating the control board and can manage yourself to a quite immaculate peak while additionally being as delicate as you need. Good wishes!

2. From the behind.

This one is great and is definitely not hard to pull off while pregnant since you have lots of grounded extremities for help so you can pressure less over balance and wrinkle.

One note: If you discover this position causes back torment, use it sparingly. We have a great deal of different continues ahead this overview on the off chance that you need to switch things up.

3. Reverse cowgirl

The clitoral incitement is off the diagrams here because you're the one holding the reins, cowgirl. Everything you do is (delicately) jump on top and pivot, so you're facing your partner's feet. Presently your goods are facing your partner while you ride on.

Leaning forward or in reverse allows you to hit the spot, any place it might be. Simply clutch, your partner's legs or knees for help. Cheerful path!

4. O.G. oral

No extravagant maneuvering, no straining. This fan most loved needn't bother with entrance to make some great memories. Oral incitement is useful for all trimesters and gives you a lovely chance to lay back and block out. Get it, young lady.

5. Spooning

Spooning isn't only for, er, spooning. Lying on your side methods, you're pleasant and agreeable while your midsection is off the beaten path.

Because of its delicate nature, this one is most likely best when your abdomen is at its greatest — cuddling while at the same time, sex? Not an awful BOGO.

6. Anal

Wager you figured this one wouldn't make the rundown. That is the place you're off-base, kiddo.

There are some standard procedures, however...

What you'll require:

• a great splashing of lube

• a considerable lot of foreplay to get things heated up

• a condom (to avoid STIs and microorganisms)

Check your rundown and appreciate it! Simply make certain to go slowly and simple from the outset. This one is ok for all trimesters, yet you'll have to continue with alert.

Best practice for anal methods no transferring of hands, toys, tongues, or penises from goods to vag. Swapping like this can be muddled — truly — and can convolute your pregnancy.

7. Standing up

Feel free to incline toward a divider to test this one out. Standing up style or position is fun in the first and second trimester. However, you may get a little crapped in this position when your stomach becomes greater.

Simply stand with your hands on the divider and spread them (like you're being searched). This is a decent method to get some help, and it makes for too simple access to be taken from behind. It's a decent pretend open door too. Think about a cop cap and sleeves.

8. Situated/seated

Sit down! This one justifies itself with real evidence, and you have two or three choices.

1. While your partner sits any old were (likely on the edge of some durable furnishings), sit facing ceaselessly from them. Presently you're both agreeable, and your partner's hands are allowed to meander. This is a decent time to have your bosoms or clit stroked.

2. You sit someplace happy with, facing your partner, and let them do their thing.

Either alternative conveys max fulfillment while you unwind and appreciate the ride. Pull up a seat, sister.

9. Next to each other

This one is sweet and romantic. You and your partner lie facing one another, and one of you swings your leg over the other. You're your ally (again, so agreeable), and you can keep one leg directly to get a pleasant edge moving.

Don't hesitate to look profoundly into one another's eyes, since you're up close here while staying comfortable in bed. Too charming.

10. Scissor

This move is as delicate as a sheep. If your legs are intercrossed, this style position makes for more slow infiltration, which you may value during increasingly delicate or sore occasions. Still sexy, still takes care of business.

11. Tabletop

This one is beyond comfortable. Simply rests with your goods on the edge of a bed, love seat, table, whatever, and have your partner bolster your legs by holding them on either side of their body while standing.

They enter from this position and blast — you're both agreeable and good to go. It's a win-win.

12. Kneeling reverse cowgirl

Ride them, cowgirl (again). With this style this time, your partner is kneeling (instead of lying down) while you recline onto them, reverse cowgirl-style. This implies little weight on your back, and pleasant progress moves into doggy style (in the event that you were looking for one).

13. Edge of want

This move makes them chill on the edge of a bed (or futon or whatever — you do you!), just sitting up while your partner is leaning or on their knees on the floor before you.

This involve scooping you up and bring you in pleasant and close, and you both have at it — another pleasant chance to plunk down while living your best life.

While you're gettin' occupied, avoid these moves.

There are a few moves you'll need to maintain a strategic distance from — fortunately, they're the more essential ones.

• Missionary (your partner on top). Old Reliable here can really confine bloodstream to momma and child. Hit the nap button on this one until after the child shows up.

• Anything level on your stomach. For evident reasons, lying on your stomach under any conditions, sexy time or not, will be not going to be overly agreeable or safe while you're pregnant.

• PSA: Don't blow it. While this isn't a move as such, don't let air get blown up there. At the point when your partner is servicing you orally or Otherwise, ensure they don't blow air straightforwardly into your vagina. An abrupt eruption of air can cause an air embolism, which can be exceptionally risky, even deadly (hold up).

Chapter Seven

BEYOND THE BEDROOM

Our trusty, time tested beds are truly where it's at with regards to lovemaking, and all things considered: it's a delicate surface for gettin' it on. However, in case you're not doing it in each room of your home, would you say you are truly getting the greater part of those month to month contract installments? We don't think along these lines, so here are some position thoughts that you can give a shot in more places around the house.

In the Living Room, on a Couch or a Lounging Chair

You: nestled into a ball, lying on your side with your hip propped up on the arm of the seat or lounge chair. The male partner, standing to the side of the sofa or seat, enters you from behind while you're your ally, driving down with his pushes to apply pressure on the dividers on both sides of your vagina. Pair this position with a solid and rumbly clit vibe that you'll both have the option to believe in adding some icing to this cake.

In the Hallway

Make standing-up sex positions really achievable by using the more tightly quarters gave by a door jamb. She supports her back against one side of the edge and puts her foot on the other side to keep one advantage easily, allowing the two partners to stand vis-à-vis just as serenely modify for tallness.

The Laundry Room

At the point when the washer gets to the spin cycle, she lays her stomach corner to corner over the top of the washing machine, propping one advantage to let the male partner enter from behind. Having one advantage will likewise enable her to edge her vagina closer to the corner or edge of the machine in request to exploit those profoundly thunderous vibrations. The best part? Warm towels for a post-coital tidy up, new out of the dryer!

At a Window

Partake in some partial exhibitionism by sticking the upper portion of your body out of an open (ground floor, for security) window. If your partner enters from the behind, you can lay your elbows on the windowsill. Supposedly, you're simply examining the area!

The Tub

In this situation, the inclusion of a partner is totally discretionary. A separable shower head can give warmth and predictable sensations in lieu of a waterproof vibrator. However, if you pair a separable shower head with a little, waterproof vibrator, you can wear inside your vagina? That is a match made in a dangerous, sudsy paradise.

In the Dining Room

Spread out a spread that will truly get your partner's mouth-watering! You: lying down on top of the dining room table. Your partner: sitting at the table with your feet on their shoulders. Get the image? Time to dive in! As a nourishment and-vibe pairing, incorporate a little handheld clit vibrator to up the sensations and enable your partner to concentrate on other regions.

The Backyard

This last one could be viewed as a curve for not, in fact, being *in* the house, yet on the off chance that it's on the property, it's the reasonable game the extent that we are concerned. On the off chance that you have a backyard or a back deck – even an apartment overhang – with a deck relax seat, you're in karma. Your partner can lie back on the lounger as you straddle them in a reverse-cowgirl position out in the outside and hello presto: you're having some underhanded open-air sex. Do this under the front of dull obviously and have some thought for neighbors, and wear an extra-long shirt to cover yourself for some additional security from uninvited eyes.

Man on Top Sex Positions

On the off chance that you're sexually experienced, then you likely definitely realize how man on top sex functions.

What you cannot deny is this speaks to probably the most effortless approaches to give a woman an orgasm and fulfill her genuinely into the bargain. Honestly, with the man on top sex, really, it is anything but difficult to joy a woman in bed.

The explanation? Since everybody cherishes man on top sex - it's intimate, there's loads of body contact, the man can push profoundly, and the woman regularly has a sense of security and satisfied.

Be that as it may, to help the individuals who aren't acquainted with how it functions, the man positions himself over the woman with his weight pretty much bolstered on his arms, knees, and legs, while she lies on her back with her partner's legs inside or outside hers.

There are many systems to use in this fundamental position, all of which give an alternate encounter to the man and the woman - for instance, in the event that she has her legs outside his, her vagina won't be as tight as it would be on the off chance that she had her legs inside his.

Tantric Sex

"Tantric," as applied to Tantric Sex, originates in India, where a Tantra is a composed book that would have been some kind of composed expert on sex, religion, or otherworldliness.

In the Hindu convention, the Tantra would be poured over by those wishing to accomplish edification, similarly, as a mantra, a verbally expressed serenade or petition, could deliver otherworldly illumination whenever utilized more than once and with the right profound disposition.

In this way, Tantric sex implies sex, where you adhere to a progression of instructions or writings with the object of achieving otherworldly edification. It isn't, rehash not, just about better sex; it isn't only an approach to accomplish better orgasms.though that might be an invite reaction!

The most renowned of these conceivably enlightening writings on Tantric Sex is likely the Karma Sutra. However, there are others, since other religions other than Hinduism grasped the thoughts behind the Tantras.

For instance, they offer a lot of exhortation on positions, however as we as a whole know, sex goes a long way beyond the basic demonstration of finding new physical approaches to express your craving: these writings additionally contain information on how to assemble and maintain a long haul and serious relationship.

Contorted Amazon Sex Position

Each family needs a Twist, and the Amazon is no special case. In this variety, the woman mounts from the side in a half-kneeling, half-squatting position, the combination of which might be increasingly agreeable for certain couples. With the woman being positioned for the most part on one side of the man's body, the man has significantly more opportunity to move his back leg outward, allowing for probably the deepest entrance in the Amazon family.

Amazon 180 Sex Position

Otherwise known as Reverse Amazon

A 180 curve on the standard variety, the Amazon 180 has the woman facing ceaselessly from her man. The most recognizable distinction is the extra improved space for ladies, who would now be able to bring their knees a lot nearer together and comparatively for men, who have much less weight pressing down on their legs. However, it is a lot simpler to hurt a man by leaning or sliding too far forward, so we ask a woman to be mindful of their man's cutoff points.

Planted Amazon Sex Position

The Planted variety of the Amazon family is the most dominating for ladies, making it an extraordinary candidate for couples that appreciate a little domination and accommodation activity. Given that so many positions overlay ladies up into pretzels, it's not out of the question for men to experience what it feels like! Since this position has the most measure of weight on the man, you'll definitely need to begin delayed to set up any points of confinement and be mindful so as not to pass them once things get moving.

Twisted Pretzel

Instructions Lie down on the bed on your right side and get your man to straddle over your right leg. As he slowly and gently enters you, he should wrap your left leg around his side to create a 'pretzel' shape. This position allows you to still benefit from deep penetration and eye contact.

With regard to sex, there are widespread rules that one ought to, for the most part, pursue. It's a code of manners that each Millennial ought to know about.

Tragically, very frequently, many of these rules and guidelines are overlooked or out rightly ignored, causing one of the two parties to turn out to be altogether unsatisfied with their sexual experience.

I state enough of that commotion! These rules aren't intended to undermine an individual's individuality or cause confinements in the bedroom;

they're there to ensure that the two parties feel similarly regarded, agreeable, and content.

Sex is an awesome thing that is incredibly charming, yet once in a while, things escape hand. Possibly you're only corroded on the rules, or perhaps you've blanked on them totally.

Either way, here are 22 legitimate, implicit sex rules everybody should know (and strictly pursue) on the fly:

1. You can't get what you don't request.

And genuineness is the best strategy. If you don't request something, your partners are not minded perusers - you can't expect that they'll recognize what you need.

Certainly, you risk there not being down with the grimy, yet it's smarter to have attempted and fizzled than to have never attempted. Also, in the event that they state "yes," you're free for next time, too.

2. Try not to hope to get activity down beneath without being willing to dive in, too.

Sex is about to give and take. In case you're going to get it, be eager to give it. Presently, in the event that one of you just wants to do it and just goes for the main occasion directly after, that is fine too.

3. In many societies, spitting is a kind of impolite.

Tap on the shoulder is a kind signal.

4. On the off chance that your partner is doing something you're not down for, state something.

On the off chance that you don't tell your partner you're not alright with whatever position you're in, or you're not feeling great with where hands are straying, left it alone known.

5. Never drive a young lady's head down in the event that you don't need teeth.

We'll do it in the event that we need to do it. And in the event that you need it that seriously, inquire. That way, we can say "yes," or "no," without feeling compelled or awkward should we decide to disregard your undesirable advances.

6. Try not to gaze.

If you don't mind, never be that individual who gazes for an awkwardly prolonged stretch of time into your partner's eyes mid-intercourse. You don't look sexy, and you look constipated.

It feels extremely cumbersome. Without a doubt, a passionate kiss is consummately adequate, yet adhere to a five-second rule with regards to eye to eye connection.

7. This isn't the library; make some clamor.

Nothing is creepier than having sex with an individual who's quiet during the demonstration — all things considered, other than perhaps the previously mentioned individual who gazes for inappropriate measures of time.

On the off chance that you like something, let your partner know with a bit "goodness," "ah," activity. Besides, on the off chance that you give vocal insistence, you're significantly more liable to get a greater amount of the great stuff.

8. Never go after the indirect access without a dialog beforehand.

This is certainly not a "we should pull out all the stops!" kind of sexual exercise. This little game requires some investment, arrangement, and trust. Don't simply come knocking on a woman's indirect access without (and I feel compelled to pressure this as much as possible) EXPLICIT authorization.

9. Accept you will utilize a condom.

This implies continually coming arranged. Try not to think you're going skin-to-skin - particularly if this is a young lady you just met in a bar. You should think as much about her wellbeing as you do your own. Try not to play dumb.

And also, in the event that you didn't inquire as to whether she's on the pill, don't expect she is.

10. A shower isn't an invitation.

Shower sex is fucking awful. On the off chance that your partner bounces in the shower, don't you dare think that warrants an invitation. On the off chance that we women might want you to join us (however Lord just knows why in hellfire any of us would), we'll make certain to tell you.

11. Try not to accept that you're spending the night.

Women and honorable men, in light of the fact that sexual relations took place, doesn't mean there is an inferred sleepover. This particularly goes for a one-night stand. Beset up to really try to understand and get a taxi home.

Fellows, consider the young lady a taxi in the event that you don't need her to remain. She let you see her exposed, and it's the least you can do.

12. In the event that you choose to run the red light, don't stop at the intersection.

In case you're going to state you're fine with some strawberry and cream, don't pull out last-minute acting all earned out. It's a characteristic thing that happens to our womanly bodies, in spite of how heartbreaking that might be.

Simply recollect, towel down before you get down.

13. No pregnancy jokes.

Yet, it is significant that you two know where you stand should the circumstance emerge.

Have an arrangement set up that you two are alright with. And I think this abandons saying, yet don't discuss this "plan" while bare.

14. The morning-after pill.

Fellows, you pay for it, and you take her to get it. Be a gentleman. Or if nothing else offers to pay. I she needs to part, it's debatable.

15. No Tindering in the wake of pulling out.

Your dating applications can hold up until only you're. On the off chance that they can't, I would recommend seeing a pro since you plainly have a fixation. And while you're busy, you should get tried for STDs.

16. You can generally help tidy up.

Get the woman a towel.

17. If you can't recollect your partner's name, simply don't utter a word.

Try not to imagine... simply keep your mouth shut. Odds are, your partner most likely doesn't recollect either.

18. Foreplay isn't "discretionary."

Your head may escape from you, however, recollect, in the event that you'd prefer to go for adjusts two and three, you have to back the f*ck off and plan.

19. In the event that you went through the night, offer breakfast.

On the off chance that you've remained the night at somebody's place, constantly offer to purchase or make breakfast. It's remuneration, brother.

20. Keep it out of the woman's hair.

On the off chance that I've said it once, I've said it a thousand times: Do not shoot your swimmers into our hair. We likely invested a ton of energy, making it look pretty. Thus the current bare circumstance we're as of now in — point, buster, point.

21. No getting earned out before breakfast breath in the event that you initiate morning sex.

On the off chance that you didn't brush your teeth, you're asking for morning breath, so simply disregard it and go forward. You're both similarly net at this moment, so it shouldn't be a lot of an issue.

22. In case you're interested, request a number.

This goes for both folks and young ladies. Women, in the event that you like this man, it's impeccably fine to request his number. And fellows, don't simply leave us hanging on the off chance that you need to see us again. You won't get another opportunity in the event that you have no real way to reach us.

In this way, request a number, and perhaps we can expose wrestle again at some point sooner rather than later.

How to last longer in bed is an inquiry many men are interested in as they scan for ways please their sexual partner. The examination certainly appears to propose bunches of folks are interested in this topic. I you are a person who is wondering how you can last longer in bed normally, you have gone to the opportune spot.

Truly a large number of men every year battle with performance issues. And we should be genuine – most folks need to abstain from reaching for doctor-prescribed medications, such as Viagra and Cialis, in the event that they can support it.

So what are the manners in which you can last longer in bed normally? Is there truly anything you can do to stretch the experience? The appropriate response is total, yes!

Last Longer in Bed

Before you have a go at anything in the regular sense to last longer in bed, it is significant that you preclude any previous ailments that might be contributing to your intimacy burdens. You may be s to realize that even generally minor issues, for example, a cold, can affect performance.

And so before you take a stab at any of the ten recommendations made here, ensure you get looked at by your doctor. In the event that you are taking any meds, remember that a few medications totally can cause difficulties in the bedroom. This is particularly valid for against sorrow meds.

Alright – since we have that off the beaten path, would you say you are prepared for the 10 proposals on how to last longer in bed normally? How about we hop directly in!

1. Become increasingly mindful of touch

Mindfulness is a topic that has been discussed before on this blog. Being increasingly mindful of your partner is principal to lasting longer in bed normally. This implies having a total focal point of what's going on inside of you and your surroundings.

2. Edging

Edging is a 25-penny term used to depict the customary "star-stop" strategy. Basically, when you feel yourself going to discharge, stop. This sets aside some effort to adapt, so don't expect results right away. In the event that you delight yourself, you can figure out how to rehearse this a piece without anyone else. Keep in mind, lasting longer in bed is scholarly conduct.

3. Stop watching grown-up video

One reason folks make some hard memories lasting longer in bed is a result of the requirement for visual incitement. Let's be honest – we men are visual folks. With that mutual, in the event that you have gotten subject to obvious signals in request to perform, you are making it practically difficult to get mindful of the other individual and "last." Periodic video watching is OK every now and then yet not in the event that it implies you require advanced symbolism in request to "man up" as it were!

4. Utilize sensate core interest

The act of sensate center (SF) was introduced in the 1960s by Masters and Johnson. At its center, SF is the act of touching a partner in an arousing path without completing the deed through extreme discharge. Using mindfulness, you essentially become invigorated by experiencing various parts of your partner's body and, consequently, allowing them to do likewise. Afterward, by using edging has examined above, you experience each other all the more intimately.

5. Take part in work out

Stamina is an undeniable part of lasting longer in bed. Stamina, however, can't occur except if the continuance is part of the condition. Pick a work plan that most intently pursues your objectives and way of life. And it is imperative to state here that maintaining a solid weight has an effect on how you perform behind shut entryways.

6. Concentrate on your partner first

Surprised, you may need to escape your usual range of familiarity and by augmentation, routine, and spotlight on making your partner orgasm first. This doesn't imply that you won't encounter an extreme discharge. It does, however, imply that you will be taking the weight off yourself to perform. Assess how things have historically streamed and make a change around there if conceivable.

7. Change areas

Once in a while, individuals contract an instance of the "regular old-same olds." This implies in the event that you have been doing it in a similar area, again and again, and the dynamic has likely gotten stale. Take a stab at something extraordinary. Intimacy doesn't need to be confined to the bedroom. There are heaps of other spots for this to occur. Utilize your imagination a piece.

8 Eat more foods grown from the ground

It's a well-known fact that foods grown from the ground contain nourishing supplements and vitamins. What you cannot deny is that you are helping yourself last longer in the bedroom when you eat these kinds of nourishments all the time. Great decisions include bananas and strawberries.

9 Reduce sugar intake

The well-known adage, "What goes up, must descend" is totally valid. While this might be a rough representation, actually sugar increases your vitality level and by expansion. Inevitably, that sugar buzz is going to leave, sending you and your Johnson descending. Sugar crashes likewise leave you drained of vitality.

10 Get a lot of rest

At the point when we are drained, we are increasingly on edge. This isn't actually the sort of spot we need to be in the event that we are looking for approaches to last longer in bed normally. As a rule, attempt to get 8 hours of rest every night.If you can't get in 8, target something like 7. An absence of shut-eye completely can affect how you act in the bedroom.

Chapter Eight

EXERCISES TO INCREASE MALE ORGASMIC CONTROL

Male Multiple Orgasms: Techniques, Approaches and Exercises

What pursues is a synopsis of a portion of the systems exhibited in The Multi-Orgasmic Man. Remember this is only a small amount of the information exhibited in the book: a great deal of supporting material is forgotten about, alongside ALL the material identified with "vitality" strategies. In particular, this rundown will see you through just the initial segment of The Multi-Orgasmic Man: on the off chance that you like what you experience depends on the material beneath, then by all methods purchase the book and attempt the rest.

The Basic Approach

This current book's essential methodology for male multiple orgasms is that men stop or change the incitement they are creating/receiving only before reaching the point of ejaculatory inevitability. Whenever done close enough to discharge, one may encounter the solid withdrawals that go with what the creators call "contractile stage orgasms" without moving into "ejection stage orgasm." Expulsion-stage orgasm is joined

by discharge and erection misfortune, while contractile-stage orgasm is joined by the typical feelings of "coming" (including the 3-5 sec. "flutter-
ing" strong constrictions in the pelvis) without
discharge and without erection misfortune.

The Multi-Orgasmic Man proposes that men
"top" to this contractile stage orgasm many occasions through the span of a lovemaking session or
masturbation session. Subsequent to experiencing every orgasm, one stops for a couple of moments and then continues whatever pleasurable
incitement one was occupied with.

Legitimate Breathing

The initial step this book examines is learning
about breathing. By breathing profoundly and
consistently (without hyperventilating), one can
gain more control over orgasm, and improve

one's capacity to skirt along the contractile side of things without falling over into the exclusionary side of things. Here's how to rehearse:

Exercise 1

1. Sit on a chair or sofa with your back straight up and your feet touching the floor about shoulder-width apart.

2. Place your hands over your navel and loosen up your shoulders.

3. Inhale your nose, however, and feel your lower mid-region expand at the navel region (underneath and around it) with the goal that it swells outward. Your stomach will likewise drop.

4. Keeping your chest loose, breathe out with some power to pull the lower stomach area back in, as though you were pulling your navel back

toward your spine. Likewise, feel your penis and balls pull up.

5. Repeat stages 3 and 4 eighteen to thirty-six times.

Learning to Focus Attention

The following activity upgrades the capacity to focus. The capacity to focus on one's partner is a significant part of sex.

Exercise 2

1. Slowly inhale (expanding your paunch) and breathe out (flattening your stomach). Tally each total inhalation and exhalation as one breath.

2. Continue breathing from the paunch and counting from balanced hundred, thinking just about your breathing.

3. If you notice that your mind is not focused, start again.

4. Repeat this activity two times per day until you can check to one hundred easily.

Finding the PC Muscle

The PC (pubococcygeus) muscle is liable for the musical constrictions in the pelvis and rear-ends during orgasm. In ladies, PC muscle compressions might be utilized to contract around the penis, causing further incitement. In the two people, a solid PC muscle is related to more grounded orgasms. Other than this impact, cognizant withdrawal of the PC muscle around the prostate gland is one system this book prescribes men use in helping to maintain a strategic distance from discharge.

Exercise 3

EXERCISES TO INCREASE MALE ORGASMIC...

1. When you are going to urinate, stand on your toes and the chunks of your feet. On the off chance that important, you can utilize the divider for help.

2. Inhale profoundly.

3. Breathe out step by step, intensely push out the pee while pulling up on your perineum and grasping your teeth.

4. Breathe in and contract your PC muscle to stop the movement of pee midstream.

5. Exhale and start urinating again.

6. Repeat stages 4 and 5 three to multiple times or until you have finished urinating.

Strengthening the PC Muscle

This activity is intended to strengthen the PC muscle. Albeit one could possibly stop doing exercise 1 when appropriate breathing turns out to be natural during sex, and one could stop doing exercise 2 when one is fit for directing and maintaining consideration, and one could stop doing exercise 3 when one knows about one's PC muscle, one should make a propensity for doing exercise 4. The more it is done, the more grounded the PC muscle will get, and the better sex will feel.

This activity may likewise be finished by ladies to get comparative advantages. It will be ideal if you note that in the activity beneath the main extremely significant withdrawal is the PC compression. You may skirt the mouth and eye withdrawals on the off chance that you wish, just as any pelvic compressions random to the PC muscle.

Exercise 4

1. Inhale and focus on your prostate, perineum, and butt.

2. As you breathe out, contract your PC muscle around your prostate and around your butt while simultaneously contracting the muscles around your eyes and mouth.

3. Inhale and unwind, releasing your PC, eye, and mouth muscles.

4. Repeat stages 2 and 3, contracting your muscles as you breathe out and releasing them as you inhale, nine to thirty-six times.

Self-Pleasuring

This is the place the center strategy of male multiple orgasms is found out before they're incorporated into lovemaking with a partner.

Exercise 5

1. Start by lubricating your penis. The ointment will increase your sensations. Oil is commonly superior to moisturizer, which evaporates all the more rapidly. [Though remember this is only for self-pleasuring - for sex with a partner, the oil will separate latex condoms, and isn't the most advantageous thing for the vagina, so it's not what you'd need to use with a partner.]

2. Remembering to massage and invigorate your whole penis, your scrotum, and your perineum, including what the book calls the "Million-Dollar Point" (a point on the perineum simply forward of the rear-end). Continue to breathe profoundly and normally, as you learned in practice 1.

3. Try to see your increasing degrees of excitement: notice the tingling at the foundation of

your penis, notice the phases of erection, notice your pulse rise.

4. When you are getting close to discharge, stop and rest (perhaps breathing in profoundly and holding the breath for a second or two). Attempt to see the compression of your PC muscle and rear-end that happens at contractile-stage orgasm, despite the fact that it doesn't be amazed on the off chance that it requires some investment to encounter this without ejaculating. You can likewise attempt to press your PC muscle around your prostate if the prostate beginnings are contracting, and you are apprehensive you may fall over the edge.

5. After you regain control, you can begin the same number of times again as you like and continue for whatever length of time that you like.

In this activity, one should explore different avenues regarding getting as close as conceivable to discharge without ejaculating. The PC muscle withdrawal part of this method is the thing that enables you to get MUCH nearer to discharge (and thus experience a full non-ejaculatory orgasm) than unimportant stopping would permit.

In the event that you manage to accomplish contractile-stage orgasms (without ejaculating) twice or more in one masturbation session without losing your erection, then you should praise yourself: you're multi-orgasmic!

Incorporating Multiple Orgasms into Sex with a Partner

When the best possible feelings are recognized and experienced in Exercise 5 (withdrawals of the PC muscle that WOULD have prompted discharge yet don't depend on the grounds that you stopped and/or cinched your PC muscle around your prostate) they can be diverted over straight into sex with a partner. The main contrast is that with a partner, you for the most part stop thrusting or something bad might happen (verbally or non-verbally) request that your partner delayed down/stop anything that THEY are doing rather than slowing down/stopping your very own hand as you did in Exercise 5.

Note that in sex with a female partner, it's regularly a smart thought for the woman to encounter an orgasm or two first (manually or orally), so any stopping/starting isn't as disturbing, and so the intercourse, by and large, is progressively pleasurable. All things considered if it's vital for the man to back off to abstain from ejaculating, yet the woman is near orgasm and doesn't need thrusting to stop, there are a couple of choices. Clearly, the man can stop thrusting and massage the clitoris or vagina with his hand. Another methodology is to change the thrusting style simply: instead of moving in and out, while right in go all over or in circles while pressing your body against her clitoris. This development is driven by the pelvis and can be a ton of fun.

Choosing a Sexual Position for Intercourse with a Female Partner

"Man on Top" (teacher) position permits the great eye to eye connection, which is significant if the two partners are multi-orgasmic, and they need to do a portion of the "vitality" stuff referenced in this book. Despite the fact that this position isn't the best at enabling G-spot incitement, this kind of incitement can be increased by putting a pad underneath the woman's hips, or by her bringing her advantages to wrap over the man's shoulders (additionally, the higher the legs, the more profound the infiltration).

"Woman on Top" (straddling) position is a simple one for men to control discharge in. Gravity aids ejaculatory control, and in light of the fact that the man can loosen up his pelvic muscles, it's MUCH simpler for him to focus on what's happening and moderate things down if the discharge is too close. This position additionally enables the woman to invigorate her clitoris during sex. The way that the woman can control rate and sort of incitement, and the way that she can invigorate her clitoris during sex, make this position a generally simple one for multi-orgasmic ladies to be multi-orgasmic in.

"Man from Behind" (doggie) position is great if solid incitement is wanted, or if they want is flagging. Profound infiltration is extremely simple and becomes further the more "forward," the woman twists (for example, leaning into the bed with the legs and torso at a more honed point to one another). Clitoral incitement is simple, and G-spot incitement is truly immediate. The neglegence of eye to eye connection is the main genuine disadvantage. However, ifyou have a mirror by the bed, you can see each other's eyes by looking to the side into the mirror (which a few people find suggestive).

In case you undoubtedly peruse a huge number of kindle books promising the "best sex positions" to accomplish male and female orgasm, this is the best book to peruse. Superficially, this may appear to be an innocuous — even supportive —

sexual assistance piece. Some may even consider it to be empowering. In any case, if you look further, it's one more case of prioritizing the sexual delight of the two people.

To be clear: This digital book I'm referring to address explicitly (regularly) heterosexual, penis-in-vagina intercourse, which, lamentably, is still broadly observed as the pinnacle of sex acts, with the end being the orgasm of the individual with the penis.

This is something that has coolly considered for quite a long time, this digital book obviously points to the best sex position in history for couples, The Complete Guide of Sex for Men and Women, to Explode Your Sexual Energy, Improve your Sexual Health, Intimacy and Desire in Marriage, Tips for Pregnancy, Beginners and Advanced Sex Addict.

sexual assistance piece. Some may even consider it to be empowering. In any case, if you look further, it's one more case of prioritizing the sexual delight of the two people.

To be clear: This digital book I'm referring to address explicitly (regularly) heterosexual, penis-in-vagina intercourse, which, lamentably, is still broadly observed as the pinnacle of sex acts, with the end being the orgasm of the individual with the penis.

This is something that has coolly considered for quite a long time, this digital book obviously points to the best sex position in history for couples, The Complete Guide of Sex for Men and Women, to Explode Your Sexual Energy, Improve your Sexual Health, Intimacy and Desire in Marriage, Tips for Pregnancy, Beginners and Advanced Sex Addict.

CPSIA information can be obtained
at www.ICGtesting.com
Printed in the USA
BVHW030005070922
646316BV00011B/578